SAMUEL SEBASTIAN WESLEY

A FEW WORDS

ON

Cathedral Music and the Musical System of the Church,

WITH A

PLAN OF REFORM.

BY

SAMUEL SEBASTIAN WESLEY,

MUS. DOC.

"As there never was a National Religion without Music of some kind or other, the dispute about that which is most fit for such solemnities, is reduced to one short question: If Music be admitted into the Service of the Church, is that species of it which the most polished part of mankind regard as *good*, or that which they regard as *bad*, the most deserving of such an honour?"—BURNEY.

LONDON:
F. & J. RIVINGTON, ST. PAUL'S CHURCH YARD,
AND WATERLOO PLACE,
T. CHAPPELL, 50, NEW BOND STREET.
LEEDS:
RICHARD SLOCOMBE.
1849.

SAMUEL SEBASTIAN
WESLEY

Donald Hunt

Border Lines Series Editor
John Powell Ward

SEREN BOOKS

SEREN BOOKS is the book imprint of
Poetry Wales Press Ltd
Andmar House, Tondu Road
Bridgend, Mid Glamorgan

The Text ©Donald Hunt, 1990
The Series Preface ©John Powell Ward, 1990

ISBN 1–85411–036–5
ISBN 1–85411–037–3 paperback

Cover Painting of Samuel Sebastian Wesley by William Keighley Briggs,
by permission of the Royal College of Music

*The publisher acknowledges the financial support of the Welsh Arts
Council*

Typeset in 10½ point Plantin by Megaron, Cardiff
Printed by Billings & Sons Ltd, Worcester

Contents

Series Preface

The Border Country is that region between England and Wales
which is upland and lowland, both and neither. Centuries ago kings
and barons fought over these Marches without their national
allegiance ever being settled. In our own time, referring to his own
childhood, that eminent borderman Raymond Williams once said:
"We talked of 'The English' who were not us, and 'The Welsh'
who were not us." Even in our mobile and crowded age, the region
retains its mystery.

In cultural terms too the region is as rich and fertile as is its
agriculture and soil. The continued success of the Three Choirs
Festival and the growth of the border town of Hay as a centre of
the secondhand book trade, have both attracted international
recognition. The present series of introductory books is offered in
the light of such events. We attempt to see writers as diverse as
Mary Webb, Raymond Williams and Wilfred Owen in the special
light — perhaps that cloudy, golden twilight so characteristic of the
region — of their origin in this area or association with it. There
are titles too, though fewer, on musicians and painters. The
Gloucestershire composers such as Samuel Sebastian Wesley, and
painters like David Jones, bear the imprint of border woods, rivers,
villages and hills.

How wide is the border? It is two, five or fifteen miles each side of
the boundary; it depends on your perspective, on the placing of the
nearest towns, and on the terrain itself. It also depends on history.
In the time of Offa and after, Hereford itself was a frontier town,
and Welsh was spoken there even in the nineteenth century. True
border folk traditionally did not recognize those from even a few
miles away. Today, with greater mobility, the crossing of
boundaries is easier, whether for education, marriage, art, or
just leisure. For myself, who spent some childhood years in

Herefordshire and much of the past ten crossing between England and Wales once a week, I can only say that as you approach the border you feel it. Suddenly you are in that finally elusive terrain, looking from a bare height down on to a plain, or from the lower land up to a gap in the hills, and you want to explore it, maybe not to return.

The elusiveness pertains to the writers and artists too. Did the urbane Elizabeth Barrett Browning, just outside Ledbury till her late twenties, have a border upbringing? Are the 'English pastoral' composers, with names like Parry, Howells and Vaughan Williams, English, or are they indeed Welsh? One wonders whether border country is now suddenly found on the English side of the Severn Bridge, and how far even John Milton's *Comus*, famous for its first production in Ludlow Castle, is in any sense such a work. Then there is the mysterious Uxbridge-born Peggy Ann Whistler, transposed in the 1930s into Margiad Evans to write her visionary novels set near her beloved Ross-on-Wye and which today still retain a magical charm. Further north: could Barbara Pym, born and raised on Oswestry, even remotely be called a border writer? Most people would say that the poet A.E. Housman was far more so, yet he virtually never visited the county after which his chief book of poems, *A Shropshire Lad*, is named. Further north still: there is the village of Chirk on the boundary itself, where R.S. Thomas had his first curacy; there is Gladstone's Hawarden library, just outside Chester; there is intriguingly the Wirral town of Birkenhead, where Wilfred Owen spent his adolescence and where his fellow war poet the Welsh Eisteddfod winner Hedd Wynn was awarded his Chair — posthumously.

On the Welsh side the names are different. The mystic Ann Griffith; the metaphysical poet Henry Vaughan; the nineteenth century novelist Arthur Machen; and the remarkable Thomas Olivers of Gregynog, author of the well-known hymn 'Lo he comes with clouds descending.' Those descending clouds . . . ; in border country the scene hangs overhead, and it is easy to indulge in inaccuracies. Most significant perhaps is the difference to the two peoples on either side. From England, the border meant the enticement of emptiness, a strange unpopulated land, going up and up into the hills. From Wales, the border meant the road to London, to the university or to employment, whether by droving sheep, or later to the industries of Birmingham and Liverpool. The were alienating elements too, since borders and boundaries are necessarily political. Much is shared, yet people on each side can speak different languages, in more than one sense.

With one or two exceptions, the books in this series are brief introductory studies of a single person's work. There are no footnotes or indexes. The bibliography lists every main source referred to in the text, and sometimes others, for the use of anyone who would like to pursue the topic further. The authors reflect the diversity of their subjects. Some approach them as specialists or academics, some as poets or musicians themselves, some as ordinary people with however an established reputation of writing imaginatively and directly about what moves them. They are young and old, male and female, Welsh and English, border themselves or from further afield.

Samuel Sebastian Wesley (1810–1876) began his career at Hereford Cathedral (where his best-known anthem and hymn were written) and ended it at Gloucester. His influence on the Gloucestershire-born composers Hubert Parry, Herbert Howells and Ralph Vaughan Williams, and his unforgettable personal presence at Three Choirs Festivals, thus associate him with the area. Yet in the present study Donald Hunt treats Wesley as the much wider national figure that he also is. Hunt gives full attention to the Exeter, Leeds and Winchester years, and summarizes Wesley's life and unique revolutionary influence on English cathedral music with the insight that comes from his own years of experience in that tradition. Donald Hunt's section on Wesley's work itself is an authoritative yet equally personal account of those haunting anthems, canticles, hymns and other compositions; and his picture of Wesley's eccentric mode of living and his stormy relations with somnolent cathedral prelates makes a gripping and often very amusing story.

Donald Hunt was himself a chorister at Gloucester Cathedral and organist at the renowned Leeds Parish Church, and is now Organist and Master of the choristers at Worcester Cathedral. Publication of his book coincides with the event of the Three Choirs Festival at Worcester this year (1990) under his direction. It was also marked by the opening service of the Hay Literary Festival, consisting entirely of Wesley's music, and sung by the choir of Worcester Cathedral in the rather different setting of St Mary's Church, Hay-on-Wye, again under Donald Hunt's direction. It was a highly moving experience.

John Powell Ward

SAMUEL SEBASTIAN WESLEY

1.

His Life

I am much honoured by the invitation to write about Samuel Sebastian Wesley, who has been an influence through most of my own career, which has similarly been primarily devoted to church music.

As a young chorister at Gloucester Cathedral I experienced his ever-present disapproving glances from a fading photograph in the Song School and, later, as assistant organist it was a humbling experience to play from the same organ loft that he had frequented. It is perhaps not surprising that my earlier attempts at composition were claimed by my detractors to have been 'lifted' from the works of S.S. Wesley! When my career took me to Leeds Parish Church I felt the power of his influence even more, for the very strength of the musical tradition there could be directly attributed to his association with this great place of worship. There are even some who claim that his ghost is there when his music is sung. To find yourself only eighth in line from the "good Doctor" was a salutary experience for a young musician at the start of a career.

My ultimate move to Worcester Cathedral completes the circle. Wesley had made his mark at Worcester, where his magical playing created such an impression with the young Edward Elgar, and at the Three Choirs Festival, although we hope never to repeat the eccentricities of his performances. Intensive work for commercial recordings of his music both at Leeds and Worcester have given me an even greater insight into his particular genius, and I am happy to share with readers the great pleasure and satisfaction that I have derived from researching into the life and music of this great man.

Background

A state of confusion reigned over the British religious scene in the early nineteenth century. The evangelical movement stood in direct opposition to the established church, especially in the larger towns and cities, where the 'new' Methodism was a dominant factor. The Church of England was still under the strong influence of its Puritan heritage, with an emphasis on the requirements of the aristocracy, but the evangelical movement appeared to offer more comfortable alternatives in terms of humanitarian needs, especially concern for the poor. Neglect of buildings, furniture, and standards of worship were commonplace. Rebellion against the many social self-satisfactions of the time inevitably divided the clergy and worshippers — tensions which have constantly appeared in church history, even to the present day — producing extremely unfavourable conditions for those responsible for the nurturing and growth of church music.

Into this unsatisfactory background emerged a musical genius, Samuel Sebastian Wesley, who was to devote his art almost exclusively to the benefit of Anglican Church Music.

S.S. Wesley was descended from a family of great antiquity and celebrity. Their pedigree has been traced back to Guy, who had been made a thane by Athelstan in the middle of the tenth century; another branch of the family had been early settlers in Ireland. One ancestor had borne the Royal Standard before King Henry II during the wars in Ireland in 1172, and another had made a name for himself during the Crusades; there is also evidence of a blood relationship to the Duke of Wellington. But it was his more immediate ancestors who had brought the greatest distinction to the Wesley name. The English divine, John Wesley (1703–91) was his great uncle and the hymn writer, Charles Wesley (1707–88) was his grandfather, both of whom had an interest in music. The dawning of the romantic movement led people into into a spirit of adventure and the two great Wesleys, by their literary, preaching and administrative abilities, were to encourage a high-minded spiritual emphasis and down-to-earth impetus in making life better for their fellow beings. This was the essence of the Weslyan revival, a revival that was to have far-reaching effects on the future of the church in Britain as well as the music that it embraced.

Charles, Jnr (1757–1834) and Samuel (1766–1837), the two sons of Charles, were outstanding musicians, both showing prodigious talent from an early age, especially the latter. Their father had brought the boys to London from his Bristol home and they were soon giving public concerts, mostly at their new dwelling in Chesterfield Street, Marylebone. Both boys appeared to be highly strung, Charles displaying unusual eccentricity, while Samuel's behaviour bordered on the manic. This combination of brilliance and instability was to make Samuel unpredictable both in his musical and his family life. A career in music, however unwise that might have appeared at the time, was to be his destiny.

Samuel showed such amazing promise that even at a tender age of eight his *Eight Lessons for Harpsichord* had been published. He was reputed to be the finest performer and improviser of his day at the keyboard; he was fanatical and knowledgeable about the music of J.S. Bach, being in no small way responsible for its recognition in Britain in the early part of the nineteenth century; nor can it be overlooked that he was a prolific composer of symphonies, overtures, concertos and sonatas. Church music formed only a smallish part of his output, most of it written for the Roman Catholic Church of which he became a member in 1784, although that membership was somewhat unpredictable. We are still discovering the genius of this enigmatic man, whose music had been written between spasmodic bouts of insanity. He undoubtedly suffered mental aberrations from an early age, but his well-documented accident where he fell into a deep excavation, with resultant head injuries, will have certainly been a setback in a potentially brilliant career.

Samuel must have been an exceedingly difficult person at home. He was briefly married, but his wife, Charlotte, soon left home as life became progressively intolerable, and he wasted no time in 'setting up home' with his housekeeper, Sarah Suter. The first child of their association, Samuel Sebastian, was born at a house in Great Woodstock Street, off the Marylebone Road, on 14th August, 1810, taking his father's name and the middle name of his father's hero, J.S. Bach. There were to be three other children of this strange and unlikely family — Robert, Matthias and Eliza.

Childhood

Not a great deal is known of young Samuel's early life, beyond the fact that, while he showed talent at an early age, he failed to repeat the exceptional precocity of the earlier generation of Wesleys. He attended the Bluecoat School, Christ's Hospital, at the age of six, being one of the privileged few who were allowed to join without wearing a uniform. Two years later he was admitted as a chorister to the Chapel Royal, where he came under the influence and musical guidance of William Hawes (1785–1846), the Master of the Children. In introducing the boy to Hawes, his father wrote:

> His temper and disposition I believe to be good, wanting only due discretion, and I know him to be susceptible of kindness, which, with you I am confident he will meet.

The domestic conditions for the choristers at the Chapel Royal were reputed to be deplorable, but the young Wesley escaped this, as apparently he lived at the home of his master, establishing a cordial relationship with the family. His first song was dedicated to Mrs Hawes and his first piano composition — *Introduction and Rondo* on an air from the opera *Zemire und Azor* by Louis Spohr (1784–1859) — was published at about the same time by Hawes himself, who had previously described Wesley as "the best chorister who ever came under his care". A contemporary chronicler, and eventual pupil of Wesley, Kendrick Pyne (1852–1938), records the occasion of a visit by the Chapel Royal Choir to the Chapel of King George IV's summer residence at Brighton when Master Wesley "took the soprano and leading parts in the anthem with sweet and divine effect". A few days later the golden-voiced Sebastian sang duets at a public concert in Brighton with no less a personage than the great Italian composer, Gioacchino Rossini (1792–1868). The King himself was so impressed with the boy's talent that he presented him with a gold watch, and on another occasion he was invited to ride in the royal carriage. It was to be the only time in his life that he moved in royal circles, although things might have been different if he had spent his working life in London, and if he had followed a more fashionable course of musical activity. During this time of his educational development things must have been unbearably difficult at home, yet his father continued to teach him organ and composition. Samuel's health often gave cause for concern, and there was even an occasion when, worried by his finances, he attempted suicide by throwing himself out of a window. The family moved house to Euston Street, but the problems with Samuel continued until 1825, by which time

Samuel Sebastian was preparing to launch his career in the employment of the church. His first appointment was organist at St James' Chapel, Hampstead Road in London.

London

During the next seven years the youthful Wesley occupied the organ stool at no less than three other London churches: St Giles, Camberwell (where he was selected from twelve other candidates); St John's, Waterloo Road (succeeding Benjamin Jacob, a friend of his father), and Hampton Parish Church, where his duties also included officiating at Hampton Court. It is not clear which of these posts he held concurrently, although in later correspondence he did admit that "there was a fuss about my holding three posts together". Certainly his work at Hampton would not have been too onerous as the rebuilt church was not opened for services until September 1831, and there is also evidence to suggest that his lack of real commitment and disregard of punctuality, which dogged him throughout his career, had already begun to be a concern. He constantly sent deputies to cover his work, although to some extent a blind eye was turned as the deputy was frequently his father, by now acknowledged as one of the most renowned and skilled executants in the land.

His work during this London period was not restricted to these churches. He appeared in concerts with his father both in London and in the provinces, a notable event being the opening of the organ in St Mary Redcliffe Church, Bristol, in October 1829. Here father and son played duets, presumably one of them being the now-familiar and finely-wrought three movement sonata by Samuel. But the novelty in the programme was a performance of Sebastian's *Variations on 'God save the King'*. Wesley Junior also dabbled in secular activities, although it is not clear how successful his efforts were in this field. He was pianist and conducted the choir in a quaint performance at a London Opera House, run by Hawes, of a comic opera adaptation of Mozart's *Cosi fan tutte*. He also combined with Hawes in a melodrama entitled *The Dilosk Gatherer*, or *Eagle's Nest*. The young Wesley composed the 'melodramatic' music for this production, but the critics gave little suggestion that the work would enhance his reputation. He also took part in events at other churches and halls, including playing the organ at the annual Lenten oratorios at Drury Lane.

His compositions at this time were somewhat limited, with a greater emphasis on songs and instrumental music than church music. However there was a *Benedictus* for four voices and orchestra or piano, a *Gloria* for similar forces, and an anthem *O God, whose nature and property* for St Paul's Cathedral; not a trilogy of works to excite hope for the future saviour of English Church Music! He was obviously leading a full and varied life in London and from his later comments would appear to have enjoyed the vitality of music making in the capital city. He also found security in life at home, in spite of the traumas that must have existed there. He would have been a great source of strength to his mother, who was rather weak willed, finding it difficult to cope in the face of the health problems of her husband and the demands of the children. But Wesley's first positive step into the Cathedral Close was at hand. On 10 July, 1832, at the age of twenty-two, he was somewhat unexpectedly appointed Organist and Master of the Choristers at Hereford Cathedral.

Hereford

Documentation tells us that S.S. Wesley was engaged by the Chapter at Hereford for a salary of £52 per annum, with an additional bonus of £8, which would be paid by the "custos and vicars"; there was an additional bonus of £40 which was 'frozen' pending the decease of his superannuated predecessor, Dr John Clarke Whitfeld (1770–1836). However, Wesley was never to enjoy this addition to his salary as he was to leave his first cathedral appointment after only three years, and before Dr Clarke Whitfeld had died.

He arrived at Hereford to find the organ under repair. He also quickly realised that he must find other work, such as teaching, in order to live even modestly. His lodgings were inadequate for his needs and, after the bustle of London, he clearly found life in the border land rather tedious, experiencing bouts of loneliness and depression. He wrote profusely to his mother, quite frequently issuing instructions on the running of the house, and on other occasions giving orders such as "go to the boot-shop and order a pair of dress shoes". The specification for the shoes was very detailed, presumably to assist with his organ playing, which was very important to him. His living conditions appeared to border on poverty, and there are frequent references to homesickness.

From time to time he did escape from his boredom into the Black Mountains, even hiring a horse to make the journey. The banks of the Wye also welcomed him. Yet his short time at Hereford did prove artistically profitable, even if the young musician was not able to appreciate it at the time. His skills at the organ were already considerable, attracting attention from further afield than Herefordshire. In contemporary times he would probably have had little difficulty in establishing a career for himself as a concert organist. Then it was very difficult to exist as an organist outside the supposed security of the church. Concert organists did begin to appear in the middle of the century, by which time Wesley was past his best and the style of performance had changed considerably to meet the demands of the new patterns of organ building.

He was also to experience his first involvement with the Three Choirs Festival, a task as formidable then as it is now, and it must be remembered that he had had little acquaintance with choral/orchestral conducting. The 'Three Choirs' Festival is the popular name for what was known as the annual Music Meeting held in turn at Gloucester, Hereford and Worcester. The Festival had begun nearly one hundred and twenty years before Wesley took up his Hereford appointment, its original purpose being the performance of religious music on a festive scale by the combined Cathedral Choirs with orchestral accompaniment. The Festivals were held in late summer or early autumn, before the serious business of winter hunting began and while the country roads were still passable for horse and carriage, indicating that it was an important event in the social calendar of the city and county nobility and gentry. Religious surroundings were soon felt to be socially restricting, so it comes as little surprise to find that secular concerts and other "grand" events were added to the programme. Records have been kept since 1724, the year in which collections were first taken to alleviate the poverty of the widows and orphans of the clergy in the three dioceses. The association of the Festival with this charity continued until very recently. The other traditional feature of Services sung by the Cathedral Choirs is still preserved, although they were gradually phased out from the responsibilities of the main choral concerts in favour of choral singers, not only from the three cathedral cities, but also from other choral centres such as London, Bristol, Cardiff, Leeds and Oxford. Since the beginning of the twentieth century the chorus has been drawn almost exclusively from the three Western Shires. The Festival has survived wars, social changes and religious movements of more than two hundred and fifty years and is now recognised for its international status, although it still retains its unique local atmosphere.

The Festival that Wesley inherited had already grown into a music meeting of considerable local and national importance, attracting "persons of quality and distinction", as an advertisement of the time tells us. Originally almost exclusively devoted to the music of Purcell and Handel, by 1834 the Festival had expanded to include diverse styles and composers, the programme largely dictated by the predilections of the organist of the host cathedral, who was — and still is — the principal conductor and artistic director. It is not evident how successful Wesley was in either role, although conducting would not appear to have been his favourite pastime. The programme of the 1834 Hereford Festival is certainly interesting, not least for a greater amount of secular music than would normally have been expected at this traditionally 'religious' event. The music of Spohr figured prominently, including music from the opera that had inspired Wesley's first keyboard work; there were liberal selections from Handel's oratorios, together with Mozart's *Requiem*, and some works by Samuel Wesley. The conductor was represented by a *Sanctus*, a *Manuscript Overture*, and a sacred song *Abraham's Offering*, which one critic noted as being "performed in a manner that seemed as if none of the parties engaged understood the composer's meaning". Wesley wrote little for orchestra at any time, which makes the Overture all the more interesting. It seems to have been well received, giving rise to the hope that here was a promising new voice who would contribute with distinction to the "cantata market" on which the British musical public thrived. Wesley did not oblige. There is some speculation that the Overture was a re-working of a one-movement *Symphony in C major and minor* which had been on Wesley's drawing board for some time. One of the features of his only Hereford Festival was Mr Edward Jones's dance band, which played on several occasions until the early hours of the next morning, encouraging the 'light fantastic toe"! Another important innovation was the change of venue for the concerts, a decision which was to have considerable bearing on the whole future of the event. This is interestingly justified in the Stewards' address to their prospective public:

> In furtherance of this view, as well as in compliance with scruples to which they willingly defer, they have concurred with the Dean and Chapter in a determination to transfer the scene of the musical performances from the choir to the nave of the Cathedral, where the more ample accommodation for the auditory, the impressive character of the architecture, and the improved sphere for the undulation of harmonious sounds, will combine to augment that unspeakable fascination which is the never-failing effect of the grand compositions selected for the occasion.

The Stewards were in effect the guarantors of the Festival and until comparatively recent times were responsible for the financial, administrative and social arrangements of the occasion. How Wesley related to these aristocratic gentlemen is not recorded, but it can be safely assumed that he would have been actively involved in the relocation of the performers at this Festival.

Wesley's appearances at the Worcester and Gloucester Festivals of 1833 and 1835 respectively were, perhaps surprisingly, as a pianist, although he did write a quartet *Millions of spiritual creatures* for Gloucester.

Clearly composition had become an important aspect in his career. It could be said that a cathedral organist had not proved himself unless he had music in publication or wide circulation, and certainly church music was deluged by hundreds of trivial efforts from these learned persons. But who ever produced such a work as *The Wilderness* for his first major contribution to the vastly enlarging repertoire? This most original work, conceived on a large canvas, looks back to the pattern of the Restoration anthem for its construction.

The term anthem is applied to a piece of vocal music sung during the offices of the church to words which have no part in the prescribed liturgy. The anthem is essentially an English musical form, giving the special character to the cathedral service; although derived from the Latin motet, it had developed along separate lines since the Reformation. It received official approval in the 1662 Book of Common Prayer through the famous directive: "In quires and places where they sing, here followeth the anthem". At first the anthem resembled the motet in construction, although the words would be in the vernacular, but as secular influences from the continent began to infiltrate the courts of the Stuarts, composers such as Blow and Purcell made dramatic changes to the design of this art form. This Restoration period produced anthems of much greater length, resembling short cantatas in that they contained solo arias, duets, quartets, recitatives (a form of elevated speech), and instrumental interludes interspersed with choral numbers.

The Wilderness contains most of these features, but there the comparison ceases, for the musical language displays the opulence of the mid-nineteenth century, together with an abundance of originality and inspiration that was rare indeed at that period of English musical history. The six sections of the anthem, making notable use of solo voices in isolation and ensemble rather in the manner of a choral concerto, cover a wide range of style and emotion and, as could be anticipated, there is an important — and difficult — score for the organ. Wesley's accompaniments are variable. It is difficult to understand why the organ is designated a dull, supporting role in so many of his anthems when he was capable of writing, and playing, such colourful, independent parts, as in *The Wilderness*. It has been suggested that the inspiration for this magnificent work came from one of the composer's many visits to Wales, and this may be true. We have no real evidence that Wesley rushed to his manuscript paper under the inspiration of scenic or physical beauty, but we do know that his exceptional talent enabled him to write inspirational music as occasions demanded it. *The Wilderness* was such a work, having been written for the re-opening of the cathedral organ at Hereford in November 1832 (Wesley mistakenly dates it as 1831 on his third edition of the anthem). Obviously pleased with his efforts, the composer decided to enter the work for the Gresham Prize, an award offered annually by the formidable Maria Hackett (1783–1874), who was devoting her energies and pelf to the improvement of conditions for young choristers and, indeed, to church music in general. Wesley himself was to become associated with the same ideals later in his life, but his first attempt to secure her prize failed. First of all the entry was late, so the anthem was held over for the following year's competition; then the now-celebrated work was rejected with heavy criticism in favour of a more acceptable trifle by John Goss (1800–80). The eminent judges, including William Crotch (1775–1847), found it clever, but not worthy of Cathedral Music, and "not likely to be heard of". The harshest words though came from no less a publication than *The Times*, which said that "it is deficient in melody, confused in harmony, full of modulation run mad" — not exactly words to encourage the young ambitious composer. He also desperately needed the five guineas prize money, for clearly his impecunious state was becoming a great worry to him. In a letter to his mother which exhorts her to collect the manuscript of *The Wilderness* if it failed to win, he writes about his desperate finances, ending: "I don't say anything about coming to town, for the expense would ruin me. I suppose you can live without seeing me yet. I very much wish I could come though".

There were other compositions. He had begun to write songs and piano music during his time in London, mostly of a juvenile, experimental nature, but at Hereford he wrote a dozen songs and some keyboard music that show increasing maturity and confidence. There are a couple of small-scale anthems and some glees, including *I wish to tune my quiv'ring lyre*, which won a prize from the Gentlemen's Glee Club of Manchester in 1832. What is probably his most famous anthem, although not necessarily his finest, was written for Easter Day, 1834. *Blessed be the God and Father* is as well known for the fable surrounding it as for its music. The choir that Easter morning consisted only of trebles and a single bass (said to be the Dean's butler), for all other adult singers had left after the early Service to sing in other churches, where they also held choir membership. In spite of these appalling circumstances for a world premiere, the anthem is still sung with much affection throughout the world-wide Anglican church. It is concisely constructed in a mini-cantata form, has splendid vocal colour and contrasts, is tuneful and, above all, sets the fine text with clarity and understanding. Yet for all this the composer formed a poor opinion of the piece, writing that it is "a little thing just made to stop the gap, and never meant for publication". Whether or not he formed this opinion as a result of an horrendous first performance we shall never know, but for once the musical fraternity proved to be more sagacious than the composer. The background to the composition of this anthem also serves to illustrate the deplorable state of cathedral music and the indifference shown towards it by the authorities.

Although we recognise the two well-known "Hereford anthems" as being very significant works in the development of the composer, as well as being milestones in the church music of the nineteenth century, they were not particular landmarks to the composer himself. Even though the distinguished Dean Merewether had been supportive of Wesley's work at Hereford, his mind had been exercised by other more important matters such as the restoration of the Cathedral and generally improving the standard of worship, and he had been unable to allay Wesley's extreme dissatisfaction with his lot there. He began to look elsewhere, with special interest in the vacant post at St George's Chapel, Windsor Castle; but it was of no avail. George Elvey (1816–93), a musician of inferior talents, was preferred, although it could be argued that Wesley's gifts and aspirations might well have been stifled by that restricted environment at that time. However, his acute disappointment was alleviated by a sudden romance. After a short courtship he married Mary Anne Merewether, the sister of the Dean and the daughter of a much respected clergyman. She was an amateur musician and a person of much sensitivity who was to be a constant force and inspiration to her husband throughout their married lives. The marriage registers at Ewyas Harold church in Herefordshire have the following entry:

> Samuel Sebastian Wesley, of this parish, Bachelor, and Mary Anne Merewether, Spinster, of the (cathedral) parish of St John in the city of Hereford were married in this Church by Licence this fourth day, May 1835. William Bowen, Vicar. In the presence of William Bowen, Junior (and) John Parry.

The marriage failed to curb Wesley's wanderlust; indeed it probably contributed to it. Later that year, on 15 August, he was appointed Organist of Exeter Cathedral, replacing the recently deceased James Paddon (1768–1835). The Chapter of Hereford accepted his resignation "in consequence of having received an engagement elsewhere", and Wesley duly left for the greener pastures of Devon and away from "the frightful melancholy that besets me at all turnings".

Exeter

The next chapter of S.S. Wesley's cloistered life does not appear to have been any more pleasurable than the first. The same concerns soon become evident: lack of money, poor standards of performance, coupled with the casual attitude of the singers, the inadequacy of the organ, the lack of encouragement from the Chapter, and so on; only Wesley was now a more assured musician and personality. He had developed an acid tongue and, through his avid letter writing, showed a good command of the language, which was to be a great asset when he took the bold step of publishing his writings later in his career. Fools were certainly not suffered gladly. To make matters worse he was becoming bald, which pleased him little. In later years he resorted to wearing a wig.

It was at about this time that Wesley began to think seriously about the shortcomings of cathedral music in general. A musician of his quality would inevitably take exception to the appalling conditions forced upon the young singers under his charge; nor could he achieve any satisfaction from the terms of employment enjoyed by his lay clerks (the adult singers of the Cathedral Choir). A young musician striving for the highest standards of music in worship must have found life at Exeter extremely frustrating, and Wesley must have doubted the wisdom of his move from Hereford at an early date. He was frustrated by an unworkable choir rehearsal schedule, which included choristers' practice at 6.30 in the morning. He was frustrated by the lack of interest or talent of his lay clerks. He was frustrated by his employers, who were downright antagonistic and discouraging. Above all he was frustrated because no one seemed to care. Presumably other cathedral organists suffered the same frustrations and indignities, but as yet only Wesley harboured any thoughts of contesting them. Undoubtedly his composing suffered, for little of note emerged from this Exeter period. There were a few short anthems of little worth, some more songs, and some unfinished sketches, the most notable of which being the great *E major Service* that would be completed in Leeds. He probably lost heart for, on arrival at the Cathedral, his efforts to introduce his Hereford anthems were thwarted by the Chapter's refusal to pay for the parts to be copied. However, a major composition was forthcoming in connection with his degree exercises at Oxford. It is thought that, because of his inability to achieve satisfaction in the church, he was casting an eye towards an academic career. Before that could be contemplated he would need to acquire suitable academic qualification, hence the application to Oxford. His abilities were already so widely acknowledged that he was permitted to proceed to the combined degrees of Bachelor and Doctor of Music. His exercise consisted of an extended anthem *O Lord, thou art my God*. This over-long and rather self-conscious anthem was first sung at Magdalen College Chapel in June 1839, after which Wesley engaged in a lively exchange of views over the submitted work with Dr William Crotch, the Professor of Music at the University. Wesley had already been offended by Crotch's disparaging remarks on *The Wilderness* at the time of the Gresham Prize adjudication, and was in no mood to accept the Professor's suggestions for "improvement" of the anthem. He conducted such a persuasive argument that his Doctorate was awarded. Dr Crotch recognised Wesley's talents so much that he wrote a rare letter of congratulation, enclosing his account for £3 for the accumulated degrees. Wesley maintained his association with Crotch and was to consult him a year later when he felt that the situation at Exeter was becoming untenable. The topic concerned a dispute with the Dean over the choice of music. Crotch's advice was as follows:

> I consider an Organist bound to play the tunes appointed by the Clergyman, tho' I regret that the latter should have anything to do with the music, tho' he ought to choose the words. When I was organist of Christ Church I had frequently to play *Lord of all power and might* [Mason], a great favourite with the majority but a most contemptible production. I consider the tunes you mention as very objectionable, but probably if that were respectfully submitted to your curate he would appoint them again, even if he still continued to like them . . . At all events we cannot compel anyone to have a musical taste or to see that we have — when they have not.

It could be predicted that Wesley would quickly become disenchanted with the organ at the Cathedral, for the distinguished instrument installed by John Loosemore (?1613–81) some 170 years previously had become a patchwork of inefficiency as a result of much tampering by a variety of builders. At first the Chapter were loathe to accept their organist's advice, but his supreme confidence in his own ability and taste eventually won the day and, under his direction the instrument was rebuilt, including the provision of pedals, by the builder John Gray (d.1849). Wesley's contempt for the Chapter's musical judgement can be ascertained from a story concerning an occasion of a special service when he played *Rule Britannia* instead of the *National Anthem*. On being reprimanded by the Chapter, the Organist replied that he was not to blame as he couldn't prevent the bellows from playing the former piece. Amazingly the Chapter appeared to have accepted the explanation!

There is little documentation available of Wesley's time at Exeter, but it does seem clear that his relationship with the Chapter was permanently strained. This undoubtedly caused him to look around for alternative employment. One post that he sought was the professorship of music at Edinburgh University, which became vacant in 1841, but once again his ambitions were dented by the appointment of someone with lesser skills, this time Henry Bishop (1786–1855). It is interesting to note that many of Wesley's competitors for advancement proceeded to knighthoods, an honour that the most significant church musician of the century was to refuse on several occasions. Even allowing for the fact that the Queen was rather over-generous in the honours that she bestowed on her musicians, it would have been appropriate if Wesley had accepted, if only to give a measure of approval to those who supported him for better standards in his chosen campaign for the improvement of church music.

Finances were an insuperable problem, but income was augmented by a profuse amount of private teaching. This did bring him into contact with many interesting people, one particularly beneficial contact being Lady Acland of Killerton. In her house was a chamber organ of such character that he was eventually moved to write two sets of *Three Pieces for a Chamber Organ* for the aristocratic lady and her musical toy. The pieces were not released until several years later, by which time they had become much broader conceptions with a larger instrument in mind.

Probably as a result of the many disappointments surrounding the work that he felt called to do, Wesley began to acquire a reputation for idleness and shelving of responsibilities on to young musicians. William Spark (1823–97), his young pupil assistant at Exeter, was to find himself more and more in charge of the music at the Cathedral, sometimes for days on end, while his master pursued his main leisure activity — fishing. An expert fisherman such as Dr Wesley, who had taken out a permit to fish in the London Docks as early as 1830, was bound to find the beautiful well-stocked rivers of Devon an irresistible lure.

His home life appeared to progress smoothly. Three of his sons were born at Exeter: John Sebastian in 1836, Samuel Annesley in 1837, and Francis Gwynne in 1841. All lived into the twentieth century, the first making a career in business, the second becoming a surgeon, the third a clergyman who also showed sufficient musical skills to become a Doctor of Music and also teach the subject at his old school, Winchester College. Francis died in 1920, leaving his whole estate and many of his father's effects and documents to the Royal College of Music. His father, Samuel, had died in 1837, but an even greater sadness in the family was the death of a baby daughter on 12 February, 1840. In a letter to his widowed mother Wesley wrote: "Our dear baby is no more. It left us last night at about twelve o'clock".

Relationships with the clergy deteriorated still more, and it is thought that these were brought to a head by one of the canons casting a slur on the work of his recently deceased father. Almost miraculously an escape route presented itself. Invited to give the opening recital on the new organ in Leeds Parish Church on 18 October, 1841, Wesley found himself totally swept up in the wave of enthusiasm exuded by the remarkable Vicar of Leeds, Dr Walter Farquhar Hook (1798–1875).

Leeds

Dr Hook, a Wykehamist and one of Britain's most eminent clergymen, had developed his own brand of liturgical thinking which he described as lying between "Methodistical and Popish absurdities". He wrote: "I blame Protestants in the Church for circulating Puritan and Presbyterian books; I blame Catholics in the Church for circulating Popish books". Hook's views were treated with much suspicion on his arrival in Leeds, but his brilliance in the pulpit and his energetic response to the challenges afforded by the rapid industrial expansion of this vibrant Northern city, gradually brought him sympathetic response from his parishioners. He caused the rebuild of the Parish Church as it stands today, taking care that every detail should be worthy of a great centre of worship.

A comparable standard of music was essential to his scheme and, although he had little musical aptitude himself, he was very ready to accept the suggestions made to him that regular choral services should be held when the new church had been built. He is reputed to have said that he would introduce a cathedral-type service, even if he was forced to go to prison for it. Leeds Parish Church had been the first place in England to introduce a robed choir into the sanctuary, records suggesting that this was happening as early as 1814; so Hook, who had "found the surplices in rags and the service books in tatters", was favourably disposed to reviving the custom and to the provision of sufficient funds to endow the musical foundation, even though this meant sacrificing an extra curate on the staff. At the end of 1841 Hook disclosed that the choral services were costing "six or seven hundred pounds a year", but he was determined to press ahead with his plans for higher standards, one of his aims being to entice one of England's leading musicians away from his organ loft at Exeter. The task was easier than might have been expected, S.S. Wesley accepting Hook's offer with almost indecent haste. He took up his new appointment in February 1842 at a salary of £200 per annum, guaranteed for ten years.

The new organ at Leeds Parish Church which Wesley had opened in the previous year had been built by Greenwood Brothers at a cost of £691, the present case — which has been described as a "weird mass of carving" — with no visible pipes, costing a further £550. The specification, which must have been one of the most comprehensive in England, is given in appendix ii. An instrument of this quality would have delighted Wesley who was at the zenith of his keyboard skills at the time of his appointment to Leeds. His fame had spread far and wide and he was much sought after as a recitalist. He had inherited a love for J.S. Bach's works from his father and, by all accounts, played them with immense skill. (He chose Bach's *Prelude and Fugue in E flat* — known as the 'St Anne' — to open the organ at Leeds.) He was also brilliant at extempore playing, much appreciated by the people of Leeds, who very soon were flocking to the Parish Church to hear his skills displayed after the evening service. He also originated the practice of introductory improvisations before psalms and anthems that had no written preface. His pupil, Stark, wrote that he "displayed genius in the highest degree and I doubt if we shall ever hear the like again". Wesley had strong views on organ design and tonal qualities, with special regard to tuning the instruments to mean temperament. It is of more than passing interest that Wesley should have been so addicted to the merits of mean tuning, declaring firm opposition to the proposed changes to equal temperament in the middle of the century. Wesley was not alone in supporting the status quo, although most of his fellow cathedral organists were rather indifferent to it all. A comment in *Philosophy of Music* by Dr William Pole (1818–1900) is of interest:

> The modern practice of tuning organs to equal temperament has been a fearful detriment to their quality of tone. Under the old tuning an organ made harmonious and attractive music, which it was a pleasure to listen to, even though it might be interrupted by a 'wolf' now and then. Now, the harsh thirds, applied to the whole instrument indiscriminately, give it a cacophonous and repulsive effect.

Temperament refers to the adjustment in tuning of musical intervals away from a natural scale so that pairs of notes are combined instead of being treated individually. In equal temperament each semitone is made an equal interval, making it easy to hear and play in any key and to modulate. Mean-tone temperament rather concentrated on making several keys acceptable to the ear, while others were scarcely tolerable, and some unusable. Wesley's dogmatic views in favour of the latter are somewhat surprising in view of the complicated modulations used in some of his works. The intonation must have sounded as eccentric as his opinions.

Apart from matters of tuning Dr Wesley was also concerned that English organs were not as well appointed as their continental counterparts, largely as a result of puritanical lack of interest, especially by the cathedral authorities.

It is rather difficult to imagine that, even by the middle of the nineteenth century, to have a pedal board on the organ was either a luxury or a nuisance, depending on how the organist responded to the challenge. There is plenty of evidence, in fact, that some cathedral organists with pedal boards never used them. As we will have observed the new organ at Hereford would have possessed pedals; hence their prominent use in *The Wilderness*. Compass of pedals and manuals was another area of organ design that elicited further assertions from Wesley. He preferred the G compass for both and wrote resolutely for it, as well as fighting many a battle with organ builders for its retention; yet, paradoxically, he was prepared to settle for a compromise situation on the organs at Leeds and Gloucester, as the specifications show. In view of the fact that the G pedal board would have rendered the playing of Bach's music all but impossible, it is quite interesting to speculate on his technical methods, especially in view of the laudatory comments on his playing of the master's scores. One technical benefit to organ playing that is enjoyed to this day can be ascribed to Wesley — the concave and radiating pedal board. Having been impressed with the continental style board at the 1851 Great Exhibition, he persuaded Henry Willis (1821–1901), the leading organ builder of the day, to adopt the concave system and also to "spread them out". Willis readily adhered to this suggestion.

As could be ascertained from the above comments, true organ music was not really possible on the English organs of the time, one consequence of which was the lack of substantial writing for the instrument. Wesley, in his inconsistency, even wrote that the instrument should merely be in good order for satisfactory accompaniment of the choir, and that a large organ in a cathedral or similar building was not really necessary. Perhaps as a result of this muddled thinking, or maybe because organs under his guardianship did not match his compositional standards, he wrote little if any music for the instrument before his sojourn in Leeds. It was here that he published his two sets of *Three Pieces for Chamber Organ*, already mentioned as having been written for Lady Acland; yet their structure would seem to have the Leeds organ in mind and, in any event, the dates of the pieces are vague. His best works for the organ are *Choral Song*, a favourite with organists, although probably performed in a modern edition that destroys the work's clarity of texture; a *Larghetto*, which is really an Air with Variations; and the finest of his keyboard works, the *Introduction and Fugue in C sharp minor*. Although there are some other undated movements for organ, none achieve the level of these pieces, which in any event have only limited value when compared with organ works being produced on the continent by such composers as Mendelssohn, Brahms, and others of lesser stature. There is a famous story of Mendelssohn (1809–47) cancelling a recital in London because the organ did not have a full pedal board, yet he was to write a series of sophisticated Sonatas involving 'German Pedals' for the English market.

Wesley was acquainted with Mendelssohn, but there is no evidence that it developed into a friendship. They would presumably have met at the time that his father and Mendelssohn were advancing the music of J.S. Bach, and they would have been in each other's company at Festival concerts, such as at Birmingham, or other musical events. There was also a limited correspondence between the two men. It is certainly known that Mendelssohn had a high regard for the compositions of the Englishman.

Wesley inherited James Hill, an Irishman, as his choirmaster at Leeds Parish Church, but he made quite sure that this was to be a short-lived arrangement and, after some months of bitterness, Hill left. Wesley had not been slow to invite his pupil, William Spark, to join him from Exeter as his assistant and, for a while, after the departure of Hill he helped with the choir training at the Church, particularly with the boys. Spark (1823–98) was to become an important figure in the musical life of Leeds, forming various musical societies and being elected the first Borough Organist. He was also a prolific author, some of his writings giving an authentic portrayal of living and working with Dr Wesley. However, his work at the Parish Church was rather less distinguished; in 1844 he was thanked for his efforts and duly replaced. It was fairly common knowledge that Samuel Sebastian was not a good choir trainer, but he could not have been happy with the Church Wardens' directive of 15 January 1844 which decreed that "Dr Wesley be offered £30 to provide a proper and competent person to instruct the boys and men". This offer was eventually raised to £60 when the post was advertised. John Harding, yet another import from Exeter, was appointed from fifteen candidates, but within a short space of time Robert Senior Burton (1802–92) is mentioned as Choirmaster. Burton stayed with Wesley and ultimately succeeded him as Organist of the Parish Church; but their relationship was an uneasy one, ending in acrimony at the York Assizes in 1852 when Wesley had sued for outstanding payment on the teaching practice which he had sold to Burton for the sum of £500 on his leaving Leeds. Wesley was not too well pleased when the court only awarded him

£100 compensation. The sum involved does throw light, not only on the amount of teaching undertaken by Wesley, but also the wealth that existed in this "grimy" city.

The Wesley family first lived at Albion Place in the city centre, later moving to the marginally more salubrious surroundings of Hanover Square. Here two more sons were born: Charles Alexander in 1843 and William Ken in 1845. The former went into the church and the latter was the second son to become a surgeon, but he died young after contracting a tropical illness in India.

The Wesleys soon felt out of place in a harsher environment than they had previously experienced. It was not just the "dingy-looking mills, uninviting shops, and huge chimneys that poured forth their miles of black smoke" that Spark so graphically writes about, but also a lack of understanding of the Northern character, which they thought coarse and lacking manners. Wesley was also beginning to develop — perhaps even knowingly cultivate — some of his father's 'character', and he was also beginning to show signs of the ill-health that was to trouble him for the remainder of his life. Although a difficult person at home and with acquaintances, he was a caring husband and father and was renowned for devoted friendship to those who understood and sympathised with his ideals. He was also much loved and respected by his pupils, especially the younger students and those who were diligent; for those he was indeed a father figure. This can be witnessed in William Spark who, if the legends can be believed, suffered so many indignities at the hand and tongue of his master, yet still returned for more 'punishment', even to the extent of following his mentor to Leeds.

Spark wrote that Wesley was thrifty, even mean, and that his humour could sometimes border on cruelty but, in spite of his rather perverse behaviour, he said that 'when he did come out in all his power, it was with the stride of a giant, dwarfing all else into littleness". He also wrote that the Wesleys were constantly expressing a wish to move away and were always complaining. As in his previous posts Wesley must have quickly become dis-illusioned, for a year after his arrival in Leeds he was again applying for the post of Reid Professor at Edinburgh, only to be rejected once more, this time in favour of Henry Hugo Pierson (1815–85), who gave up the post after only a year. Wesley failed for the third time to obtain this academic appointment and then set his sights on the vacancy at Oxford University, only to be beaten again by Bishop. It was generally accepted that these appointments were largely governed by influence and it must be assumed that Wesley's abrasive personality had robbed him of the friends that he needed to succeed in the applications. Yet he was supported by some notable musicians, including the composer Spohr, who had become a friend and supporter of Wesley. In a letter of commendation supporting the second Edinburgh application Spohr wrote:

> His works show, without exception, that he is a master of both style and form of the different species of composition and keeps himself closely to the boundaries which the several kinds demand, not only in sacred art, but also in glees and in music for the pianoforte. His sacred music is chiefly distinguished by a noble, often even an antique, style, and by rich harmonies as well as surprisingly beautiful modulations.

In spite of these private disappointments his work continued to flourish at the Parish Church, where the professional choir of committed singers would have been more rewarding to him than most cathedrals in the land. He may have had little hand in the training of the choir, but his very presence ensured an enviable standard of performance; his Leeds singers would never let him down. Dr Wesley himself said that "our service is most sublime; beyond anything heard in any cathedral". There can be no question that, in spite of his reservations of them, Wesley was much admired by the inhabitants of Leeds.

In view of the fact that the number of services at the Parish Church were limited, compared with a cathedral, Wesley was able to devote more time to extra-mural activities. These included participating in events with the Musical Society, the Philharmonic Club and the Leeds Choral Society, which he conducted from time to time. He also gave a series of lectures at the Liverpool Collegiate Institution where, in a series of discourses on choral music, he fired his first broadsides against the scandalous decline in the standards of cathedral music. Some people at last began to sit up and take notice. The clergy were not pleased.

The other bonus to be derived from a less demanding round of liturgical activity was more time and inclination for composition.

Very soon after his arrival at the Parish Church Wesley prepared and published a collection of chants for a newly pointed psalter, together with some free harmonisations of metrical psalm tunes. He couldn't resist taking the opportunity of making a few more vigorous comments in the preface on the urgent need for reform in church circles. Again the clergy were not impressed, but this was only the beginning of a bitter campaign that at this stage of the proceedings Wesley was prepared to wage through his pen in almost near isolation. His *Psalter with Chants* (the second edition has the title *A selection of Psalm Tunes*), published in 1842, contains many interesting things, although it was primarily intended for domestic use — the sort of volume that all cathedral organists compile on arrival at their new post, before they become too busy or lose their enthusiasm!

The book was advertised in the *Musical Times* as follows:

> The Psalter with Chants, Pointed — the Words and Music being printed on the same page, for the use of Choirs, by Samuel Sebastian Wesley, Mus Doc. Small Pocket Copies, 3s.6d. — Octavo Edition, 10s.6d. Quarto Edition, 14s. This work gives all the best Chants in the daily use of the Church of England, together with several superlatively good ones by the late Samuel Wesley, which are copyright.

The most significant work of the Leeds period was to follow in 1845 — the magnificent *Service in E major*. This legendary work had been sketched at Exeter, although exactly how much is not known. The proficiency of his Leeds choir would in any event have reawakened his interest in this complex piece, but the real incentive for the renewal of the composition was money. Martin Cawood, a local business man, was one of those responsible for persuading Dr Hook to bring Wesley to Leeds, and a firm friendship was to develop between the ironmaster and the composer. It was Cawood who commissioned the publication of the *Service in E major*. Like the pointing of the Psalms in the 1842 volume, the Service was way ahead of its time. It was clearly a vote of confidence in his Leeds choir, who would have relished the challenge of these complicated canticles. The 'cathedral' nature of the services at Leeds were further strengthened by this music written for them by the great man, whose influence is still strong in that unique place of worship to this very day. Leeds Parish Church is still the only parish church in the country maintaining daily choral services, sung by a choir of similar size, talent and devotion to their tasks to that of Wesley's own experience. In the 1840s the fame of S.S. Wesley and Leeds Parish Church spread far and wide.

The complete Service, which Cawood bought for fifty guineas, has settings of the Te Deum, Jubilate, Kyrie, Creed, Sanctus, Magnificat and Nunc Dimittis. It is generally considered that the Service marks the summit of Wesley's achievement. In any event it shows very notable progress in the development of this type of composition, as nothing so elaborate in design had been attempted before. The first edition was handsomely produced, provision being made for another of Wesley's notorious prefaces. Again he pulled no punches, the cathedral authorities once more being apportioned the greatest criticism. He particularly attacked apathy and musical ignorance, and was obviously still harbouring discontent at the Exeter refusal to copy his music when he wrote:

> Cathedral bodies rarely encourage (even by the purchasing of a few copies for the use of their choirs) such undertakings. Indeed, such persons seldom even condescend to notice any application made to them of the kind, a fact which may astonish those who remember the nature of our Choral Service, and how largely the Musician's Art is, twice a day, called into requisition throughout the year in every Cathedral and College Chapel in the Kingdom.

The clergy again took note and were not amused; Dr Crotch, who had received a copy of the Service from the composer, was less enthusiastic about the preface than the music, and it was also unexpectedly censured by sections of the press. Some particularly biting comments from the *Illustrated London News* suggested that "Mr Wesley may be, and indeed is a wonderfully executive organist; but he has no creative fancy beyond that of foolishly entering the ring with his betters. This is not the work of a poetical musician". Wesley's rather disparaging remarks about some of the earlier composers were also not well received. There is no evidence to suggest that Wesley was particularly worried by these poor reviews, especially as his fiercest, and longest, diatribe was still to come.

Life after the *Service in E major* continued much as before with the round of work at the Church, teaching, and a fair amount of recital work around the country, including a visit to Tavistock in 1846 which brought on nostalgia for his ancestral West country. Yet he had by now found the beauty of the Yorkshire Dales very much to his liking and he was able to find solace from his fishing expeditions, which became so necessary to his way of life that exceptional absences were now being noted. One of these angling outings was to end in disaster. Just before Christmas in 1847 he set out alone at night for one of his favourite spots at Helmsley in North Yorkshire. His encounter with a stile resulted in a compound fracture of his left leg, an injury which left him lame for the remainder of his life. While recuperating at the White Swan Hotel in Helmsley he was to write, among other things, his most beautiful anthem *Cast me not away from thy presence*. This dignified masterpiece — one of the gems of English Cathedral Music — is scored for six voices and contains some of Wesley's finest choral sonorities, particularly the passage which obviously had special significance, "that the bones which thou hast broken may rejoice". The fracture did not respond well to treatment and complications were experienced, confining him to home for a lengthy period. He would not have been a good patient, nor could his wife have coped well as she appears to have suffered from regular bouts of illness.

Wesley was able to continue his letter writing and there is correspondence with Mendelssohn on what appears to be a difference of opinion on organ design. Although it was recorded that he did not approve of Mendelssohn's music, Wesley did travel to Birmingham to hear the first performance of *Elijah*, and he included no less than four of the German composer's major works at his first Gloucester Festival. His views on contemporary music could be abrasive, but he did take the trouble to discover it, unlike so many of his church music colleagues. Several of Wesley's fine short anthems have no date and some biographers have attributed them to this fruitful period in Leeds. While it is possible that the finishing touches were applied in Leeds their style seems so far removed from works such as the *Service in E major*, perhaps suggesting an earlier date of composition. In any event he would by now be turning his attention to literary matters, for the time had come for him to deliver his most passionate attack on the state of Cathedral Music through the historic book, *A Few Words on*

Cathedral Music and the Musical System of the Church, with a Plan of Reform, published in 1849.

Earlier in that same year Wesley had decided to join with Edward Taylor, the Gresham Professor of Music, in a pamphlet *Address on Church Music*. The idea was to circulate the document and at the same time invite organists and other interested parties to attend a meeting in London. Although he was happy that others were at last taking an interest in his cause, Wesley decided that things would not move fast enough, hence the speed at which his own famous dissertation was produced. Anyway he much preferred to fight his own battle. *A Few Words on Cathedral Music* will be considered in more detail later but, taken in its historical context, it was not only courageous, but also unique in church music history. No cathedral organist, before or since, has been prepared to voice his opinions so strongly while at the peak of his career and, in Wesley's case, almost certainly hoping for advancement in his profession. The clergy should have been horrified, but it would appear that they either chose to ignore the document or to dismiss it as irrelevant rantings of a disillusioned and irascible musician. Wesley's vigorous protesting would bear fruit in due course, and it could be argued that the healthy state of cathedral music today in some way stems from his efforts, but the improvements during his lifetime were almost negligible.

Wesley's action in publishing such a vitriolic treatise at a time when he was becoming more disenchanted with Leeds would appear to show some lack of perception, for he was likely to be looking for employment from the very people that he was attacking. The test was to come sooner than he may have thought and, surprisingly, it was not to be too much of a problem. Even though he had openly not enjoyed Leeds for some time, he was still enjoying local and national prestige, and his options for future employment would seem to be limited and perhaps less rewarding. His playing was much sought after, a recital for the Birmingham Festival in 1849 being a particular 'high spot', and there is nothing to suggest that the music at the Parish Church was any less efficient than it had been. It has been said that he had serious disagreements with Hook over the ordering of the services, but there is little evidence to support this. Wesley's suspicion of the Tractarian movement was well known, but the services at the Parish Church were not really fully committed to these trends, and there is no reason to believe that Hook had lost interest in the excellence of worship through music. There may have been some interferences with policies by the Choir Committee and the Church Wardens, but the reason for the distancing of Hook and Wesley was more likely to have been caused by the former's involvement in more important matters of social concern. In his time at Leeds (he left to become Dean of Chichester in 1859), Hook had been responsible for raising money to build twenty-one churches, twenty-seven schools and twenty-three vicarages, in addition to renewing the building and the worship of the Parish Church, having to constantly deal with recalcitrant church wardens to achieve his aims. He fought a resolute battle for the poor man's rights, becoming involved in both educational and ecclesiastical reform. He was involved in the treatment and care of parishioners during the cholera epidemic, challenged the mill owners over cheap labour, achieving a measure of success, and was a principal agitator in the campaign to bring through parliament the Ten Hours Bill. Like his organist, Hook was an avid writer of letters and an enthusiastic author, and he became an important personality in the life of the city. How sympathetic he was to Samuel Sebastian's campaign is not known, but he would have admired the musician's courage and integrity.

Wesley's longing for another cathedral close in the South of England was strong, as was his desire to obtain for his sons a suitable education. The perfect opportunity presented itself at Winchester Cathedral on the death of the organist George Chard (1765–1849) at the age of eighty-four. Wesley applied and was appointed. The news was received with profound regret by the musical public of Leeds as well as the congregation of the Parish Church. A famous farewell concert was given by Wesley at the Music Hall, while the congregation of the church contributed to a leaving present of a portrait in oils, which had been commissioned from the Leeds artist and alto singer, William Keighley Briggs. The portrait reveals that Wesley was a man of average height with striking features and of a dignified presence. The *Leeds Intelligencer* was extremely complimentary of this painting of the "ablest composer of Church Music of the present age". At the same time this newspaper wrote:

> It is with much regret we are obliged to confirm the correctness of
> this statement. Whoever has heard — and who has not? — Dr
> Wesley's splendid performances in the Parish Church, in which
> music has so magnificently sustained its part as the ally and
> exponent of religious sentiment — will be fully sensible of the loss
> which Leeds is about to sustain.

So ended a strange chapter in the career of Britain's most brilliant
and volatile church musician, whose next appointment was to be
the longest of his career.

Winchester

The Dean and Chapter of Winchester were well aware of the
problems they might encounter by appointing Dr Wesley. In order
to safeguard their interests they imposed several conditions with
regard to the organist's duties and responsibilities, with a special
proviso on the matter of attendance. They could hardly be blamed
for taking this action but, at the same time, they did show
remarkable tolerance in view of his reputation; they were prepared
to exchange possible difficulties for the distinction that Wesley's
music making would bring to the Cathedral. Once Wesley had
agreed to the conditions he was appointed at a salary of £150 per
annum. On September 1st the *Hampshire Chronicle* announced
that "Dr Samuel Sebastian Wesley, son of the late eminent Mr
Samuel Wesley, has been appointed to succeed Dr Chard as
organist of our Cathedral". It is interesting to note that, twelve
years after his death, his father was still held in high esteem, and
that it appeared necessary to mention his name as if giving his son
credibility. One disappointment was the fact that he was not to hold
concurrently the post at Winchester College. The jobs had been
separated, the College post being offered to Benjamin Long,
assistant at the Cathedral and a fellow-candidate for the Organist's
appointment.

The move to Winchester appeared to proceed smoothly, the
Wesleys taking up residence in Kingsgate Street in the September
of 1849. They were to move into the Cathedral Close at a later date.

It was not long before the new organist's music appeared on the
lists, (unlike Exeter), his Leeds Service being heard as early as the
first Sunday in October. The Choir were soon to absorb other

works into the repertoire. The music of S.S. Wesley had not been accepted by Chard, who no doubt couldn't face the new techniques posed by this younger 'avant-garde' composer. It is probably true to say that acceptance of Wesley's music was slow to emerge in most musical circles at the time, although publishers were to show a healthy interest. However, at Winchester this 'new' music was readily — even enthusiastically — accepted by the choir and congregation alike, prompting the local newspaper to write:

> The reputation acquired by Dr Wesley in Leeds has been still more appreciated in this city, as manifested by increasing anxiety to witness the extraordinary talent displayed at the organ in the beautiful choral services of our Cathedral.

To be so warmly accepted into the life of the city should have been a great encouragement to Wesley, still only in his fortieth year, providing a real opportunity to compensate for the lost time in his career by moving to Leeds, a feeling that he was to express strongly in his later years. Events were to prove that he did not grasp the opportunities.

A year after Wesley's arrival in Winchester Long died, so the appointments of organist at the Cathedral and the College were once again joined, to continue a tradition that had lasted for more than a century. Of course there were obvious disadvantages of the dual appointment, not least the unacceptable disappearances of the organist from the cathedral, usually by crawling on hands and knees from the organ loft, in order to transfer to the College. There can be little doubt that Wesley soon used this same means of exit to transfer to the banks of the Itchen, another notoriously well-stocked river. At a later rebuild of the organ Wesley was allowed to have a secluded stairway in order to make a more dignified departure, even though its appearance desecrated the beautiful twelfth century chapel of the Holy Sepulchre.

At this time Wesley was much involved in organ construction, and not only with the inevitable rebuild of the Cathedral Organ. The Great Exhibition of 1851 inspired Henry Willis to produce one of his very finest organs, much admired by all discerning organists. Wesley quickly saw its potential, persuading the Dean and Chapter of Winchester to purchase a large part of it for installation in the Cathedral. Although he had expressed satisfaction of the Cathedral instrument before he had been appointed, he soon discarded his good intentions. His first strong objection was to the Gothic style organ case designed by Blore, but vociferous concern at the poor tonal quality of the instrument built by John Avery (d.1808) was not long delayed. At first the Chapter were very suspicious, one Canon Pretyman being particularly objectionable, questioning the organist's ability to give sound advice, as well as resenting the anticipated cost. Wesley was not slow to retaliate by making heavy criticism of the Canon, known to spend lavishly on entertainment, for his "Lazarus position" on the music. But Wesley won the day, the organ being duly erected during 1854 at the huge cost of £2500, much of it raised by public subscription, the Queen and the Prince Consort being among the distinguished donors. The large design of the organ posed some structural problems, causing delays to the opening ceremony; but, when the great day arrived — 3rd June, 1854 — the Cathedral was packed. The excited congregation heard a masterly display of organ playing as well as a Service consisting entirely of Wesley's compositions, including a specially written anthem *By the word of the Lord were the heavens made*, a rather ordinary piece for such a unique occasion.

Wesley's advice was being widely sought on organ construction, among his most interesting assignments being advice on the installation of the massive new organ at St George's Hall, Liverpool. As a result of the good impression created by the Great Exhibition organ, Wesley persuaded a group of committee members from Liverpool to inspect the organ on site, after which the order for the St George's Hall organ was placed with Henry Willis. Wesley opened the new instrument on 18th September 1854, giving further recitals there the following year. His one attempt to become a concert organist failed. Obviously impressed with the organ at St George's Hall, and relishing the prospect of a different life-style as a concert organist he applied to be the first incumbent of the Liverpool post, only to have his hopes dashed yet again when it was offered to the younger W.T. Best (1826–97). Yet it is doubtful if he could have successfully sustained that appointment. His playing was of the old "church style" and there is little to suggest that he had either the knowledge or the inclination to adapt to the new repertoire of the "poor man's orchestra". His own recital programmes appear very ordinary to our present-day scrutiny, and compare unfavourably with the new-style programmes being presented in the numerous concert halls which were springing up around the country. His programmes invariably consisted of a couple of major works of Bach, some of his own compositions, occasionally one of his father's voluntaries, a selection of short pieces which would almost inevitably include a trifle by Spohr, and ending with an extemporisation.

Sadly it appeared that Wesley's skills at the organ were already beginning to desert him. His accident may have been a contributory factor, but it is more likely to have been a falling off of interest, together with a reluctance to prepare himself adequately. Fortunately he retained his enthusiasm for teaching, taking on many pupils who continued in their master's style, many of them becoming leading organists of their time. He could be said to have been the founder of a school of English organ playing, rivalling that emerging from France, although of a very different type of presentation — more functional and less flamboyant. He was also able to bring his experience into a wider sphere as he had been appointed a professor of the organ at the Royal Academy of Music in 1850, although it has to be admitted that at the time that establishment was fairly moribund and unable to offer any competition to the equivalent conservatoires on the continent. It is ironic that the Wesley memorabilia should eventually be housed in the Royal College of Music, the rival establishment set up to offer some alternative to the decaying standards of the Academy.

Meanwhile he kept up his other activities, one interesting venture being a performance of *The Wilderness* at the Birmingham Festival of 1852. Wesley had written precious little orchestral music, but the opportunity of conducting one of his own works at this celebrated choral Festival, already graced by Mendelssohn and his hero, Spohr, encouraged him to orchestrate this early anthem. Unfortunately, almost certainly due to Wesley's poor direction, the work was inadequately performed and, as a result, both music and presentation received harsh criticism. Even more regrettably a quarrel followed in the press between Wesley and Henry Gauntlett (1805–76). The two had always treated each other with suspicion, mainly as a result of differing opinions on organ design, but Wesley had not really forgiven Gauntlett for his close association with Mendelssohn, culminating in his involvement at the organ in the first performance of *Elijah*. Gauntlett was also a devoted adherent of Gregorian Chant, another of Wesley's bêtes noires.

That year also saw Wesley returning to composition with another lengthy anthem *Ascribe unto the Lord*. It is interesting that, no doubt because he was involved in the orchestration of *The Wilderness*, he decided to score the new work for full orchestra as well. His only other excursions into the realms of the orchestra were to be a song and an *Ode to Labour* in 1864, the latter written for the most unlikely occasion of the North London Working Men's Industrial Exhibition. Two other fine anthems were to be written at Winchester. *Praise the Lord, O my soul* was the result of a commission to celebrate the opening of the organ at Holy Trinity Church in the city, and in the same year — 1861 — he wrote *Man that is born of a woman*, one of his most moving creations, for the funeral of the Reverend Robert Speckott Barker, Warden of the College. The death of the Prince Consort later in that year gave him an opportunity of writing a second funeral anthem *All go unto one place*, his sole example of what might be termed music for a national occasion. Some sacred songs and choruses, his first since the Hereford period, also appeared, together with a short full *Service in F major*, and also some fragments of other canticles that he would complete at his next appointment.

Several times during his career Wesley had endeavoured to arrange publication of a collection of his anthems, but each attempt had come to nothing. Following his accident in Yorkshire he made a more determined effort. An advertisement in the Leeds newspaper stated that "Dr Wesley has the honor [sic] to announce that he has nearly ready for publication, a collection of Anthems, for Cathedral Service, Composed by Himself". This was followed a few months later by an advertisement in the *Few Words on Cathedral Music*:

> Now being engraved, and published by subscription. A collection of anthems, for cathedral service, in score, with organ accompaniment. Composed by S.S. Wesley . . . about 400 copies are subscribed for. The list is still open.

All this would seem to suggest that the type was being set before the collection had been completed, as quite certainly only nine of the projected twelve anthems had been written by 1849. There followed an embarrassing silence, and it was not until 1853 that the publication is mentioned again. With the release date now in sight Wesley began to write to all the earlier interested parties in the hope of reviving their curiosity. In some cases subscriptions had been received and held for over ten years and, in giving precise details of the publication, the composer was forced to ask for additional money or offer withdrawal from the scheme in view of the time that had elapsed. He would have been specially warmed by the encouragement of his own Dean and Chapter who subscribed handsomely to the new publication. This was a noteworthy success for Wesley — a minor success for his campaign. He expressed his gratitude by dedicating the volume to his Dean, Dr Garnier. He clearly intended to publish a companion collection as it is sub-titled Volume One, but this was never to materialise. The *Twelve Anthems* extended to 270 pages and sold for two guineas. The undated masterpiece *Thou wilt keep him in perfect peace* is included in the set, which would seem to suggest that it had been written at Winchester to 'fill up' the volume. The demand for the publication exceeded expectation, causing a second impression to be issued in the following year. The Volume remained in circulation until the publishing house of Novello acquired Wesley's copyrights in 1868. Only ten cathedrals subscribed to the volume of anthems: St Asaph, Bangor, Chichester, Durham, Exeter, Hereford, Salisbury, Wells, Worcester and Winchester, the principal benefactors who purchased twenty copies. Leeds Parish Church and two each of the Oxford and Cambridge Colleges also appear on the list, as do several individuals such as Dr Hook of Leeds, with whom Wesley was supposed to have fallen out.

While at Winchester Wesley became fascinated with hymnody, spending much of his spare time composing hymn tunes and harmonising existing tunes. The reasons for this new-found interest in this very 'English' type of composition are far from clear, unless it was distaste of the many sentimental offerings of his contemporaries, especially the efforts of John Bacchus Dykes (1823–76). As the leading church musician and a man known for his intellect, artistry and unsentimental mind, Wesley was eminently suitable to set an example in the writing of hymn tunes. He also possessed good literary taste, not surprising in view of his background.

Hymn singing, as we know it, really began in the eighteenth century, and it soon became a national institution. These new appendages to the liturgy would have little effect on cathedrals for some time, as the Cathedral Offices were complete in themselves, affording little opportunity for congregational participation. Wesley had begun to express concern over the demands for greater involvement by the congregation while still at Leeds, a trend brought about by the Catholic revival in the church. This revival was based in Oxford during the period 1833–45, endeavouring to restore the high church ideals of the seventeenth century. The leaders were John Keble, John Henry Newman and Edward Bouverie Pusey. These leaders slowly influenced people to take their services more seriously; to make the communion service central to their faith; to encourage churches to ape cathedrals in their form of worship; to clutter their chancels with robed choirs and organs, and to suggest that the only real culture for the 'new' church was medieval. There was also the burning question of ritual in worship, perhaps the most contentious issue of all. All this had little effect on cathedrals at first, although they began to look with alarm at the spread of this new order. Wesley was generally hostile to the culture of these Tractarians, who looked to the melodies (Plainsong) of the ancient church for their hymnody, waging a prolonged battle over the intrusion of what he considered to be banal unison singing into the church. His most scurrilous attack against the 'Gregorians' occurred in *A Few Words on Cathedral Music*:

> Some would reject all Music but the unisonous Chants of a period of absolute barbarism — which they term 'Gregorian'. All is 'Gregorian' that is in the black diamond note! These men would look a Michael Angelo in the face and tell him Stonehenge was the perfection of architecture!

At about the same time he wrote to a pupil who had a liking for plainsong:

> Your question about Gregorian tones has caused me much pain. I thought I had made a better musician of you, I am sorry for this. I beg to assure you that I am a musician, a protestant, and yours truly, S.S. Wesley.

46

In spite of the persuasive arguments of the Oxford Movement, the Anglican Hymn continued its progress along very narrow channels. All hymns for the most part are derived from the community that they seek to serve — a type of folk music — and will inevitably reflect the language and popular styles of the day. The most successful writers and composers were not necessarily the most renowned people in their professions, but rather people who understood the prevailing mood of the time coupled with the demands of the ordinary citizen. The music was invariably simple, representing what was in vogue — that is the mawkish and sweet drawing-room ballads and part-songs. The many who enjoyed singing and listening to these creations until they "dissolved into tears" cared naught for the tasteful improvements offered by the high churchmen. To satisfy the needs of the singing congregations a new hymn book, *Hymns Ancient and Modern*, was launched in 1861.

Wesley obviously noted all this with interest and decided to jump on to the band wagon. In 1864 he arranged publication of a tune book to words by the Reverend Charles Kemble, *A Selection of Psalms and Hymns arranged for the Service of the Church of England*. This interesting book illustrates Wesley's class: the writing has a recognisable style and, although in the language of the time, has a distinctive quality placing his hymn tunes at a higher level than all but a few of the contemporary examples. Another interesting feature of this publication was that it was printed in a "cut-book system", in which the tunes were printed at the top of the pages and the words at the bottom, the pages then being horizontally sliced so that half pages could be turned separately. This system brought together any words and music for easy coalescence. Perhaps surprisingly the device was not universally used.

Wesley was pleased with his work in this new sphere of creative activity and, not only did he write many of his best tunes at this period, but he also planned the *European Psalmist*, a tome which would take him years to complete.

There is strong documentary evidence to prove that Wesley's most famous hymn tune *Aurelia* was written at Winchester. Kendrick Pyne tells the charming story:

I was in his drawing room in the Close, Winchester, as a lad of thirteen, with Mrs Wesley, my mother and Mrs Stewart (the mother of the distinguished General Stewart who fell in Egypt); we were all discussing a dish of strawberries when Dr Wesley came rushing up from below with a scrap of Ms in his hand, a psalm tune just that instant finished. Placing it on the instrument, he said, "I think this will be popular". My mother was the first ever to sing it to the words *Jerusalem the golden*. The company liked it, and Mrs Wesley on the spot christened it *Aurelia*.

This reminiscence dates the tune at precisely 1865. The composer's prediction was correct; it was indeed popular, even finding its way on to the barrel organ rolls of the period!

Dr Wesley continued to give advice to authorities on ethics, standards of presentation, quality of employment, and other matters. In his quest for improved organ design he also expressed strong views on the siting of the instrument in a cathedral context, and became involved in the question of the location of the new organ in Salisbury Cathedral. In a letter to the *Salisbury Journal* he points out the defects of placing the instrument to one side of the choir, claiming that the effects of antiphony are destroyed, that the congregations are not helped by the unbalanced sound, that the choirs cannot easily respond to the instrument and, delivering a censure on his colleagues, considered that "the defect is beyond the power of the most judicious accompanyist to rectify". In advising the authorities to place the organ in between the two sides of the choir he continues:

The profession to which I belong being rarely consulted on such a step, and knowing well, as I do, that such a step is highly detrimental to musical effect I take this means of expressing my opinion, that not only is the effect of an organ injured by being placed at the side, instead of the centre of the cathedral, but the service also suffers . . . .

His advice was ignored at Salisbury, as it had been at his own Cathedral, but he continued to speak and write powerfully on the subject.

Of course, not all Cathedral Chapters were indifferent to the musical situation which prevailed through most of the nineteenth century, and some endeavoured to improve conditions for their musicians. The advisory group, the Cathedral Commission, at least made a positive effort by sending a questionnaire to all organists and precentors, requesting personal views and suggestions on the vexed subject of music in cathedrals. There was a good written response, but Wesley felt that the cause would be best served by publishing his views in a pamphlet. So, only a short while after his *Few Words on Cathedral Music*, he was in print again in his *Reply to the Inquiries of the Cathedral Commissioners, relative to the Improvement of Divine Worship in Cathedrals*. The tenor of the argument was much the same as before, but he did make some more useful and, at the time, far-reaching suggestions. He urged that special schools should be established to train the choristers; that the organist should be a person of high qualification and experience who should be in sole charge of all matters musical; that an effective choir must have not less than twelve adult singers and, above all, that church music should be of the highest possible standard, both in performance and composition. He maintained that too much bad music was being written for the church, music that would not be tolerated in a concert hall. He was in effect anticipating Sir Thomas Beecham's famous remark that "all composers do their worst work for the church!" Wesley was again acting like the leader of a trades union for church musicians; he had the knowledge, experience and courage to speak with confidence, even if some of his own behaviour did not entirely match the ideals that he preached so forcibly. His latest pamphlet was perhaps less constructive than his previous declamations, but the old fire remained and, once again, he was to make few friends among the cathedral dignitaries, even though some were at last beginning to see some merit in his argument. The findings of the Commissioners were published in due course, but added little to what was already known, and certainly contained little of value that had not already been expounded by the 'good Doctor'.

It was to be Wesley's last published document on Cathedral Music. He maintained a vigorous interest in the subject, but no doubt felt that he could say no more. The clergy were pleased! One positive aftermath of the Commissioners' inquiry was that a deputation of cathedral organists met members of the committee, primarily to discuss the inadequacy of their stipends. Wesley joined the discontented group, but does not appear to have been their spokesman, as might have been expected. Perhaps his influence was beginning to wane?

As his decade of work at Winchester approached it would appear that Wesley had begun to lose his sparkle and enthusiasm for his work. Major compositions had become something of a rarity and, although he was still in demand as a recitalist, a younger generation was emerging with different outlooks and styles. His recital programmes were still of the pattern mentioned earlier and the Bach pieces, frequently referred to as *Prelude and Fugue*, may well have been arrangements from the '48, as an edition dated 1860 was published by Novello as 'Organ or Harmonium Music'. His extemporisations continued to be a delight, and it is interesting to quote Sir Walter Parratt (1841–1924), who had heard Wesley play at Oxford.

> Wesley used to write his subject on a little strip of music paper, and carefully place it on the desk so that he could glance at it whenever he wished. These extemporisations were sometimes almost marvellous, Wesley being especially good at 'extraneous modulation' and prone to revel in plunging into all sorts of intricacies. He was exceedingly clever in their management, and mostly came out of the fray with clean hands. He was, perhaps, the greatest extemporiser we ever had.

He still continued to write copious letters, some continuing the saga of discontent with cathedrals and his association with them, others expressing regret at ever leaving the London musical scene, and there is the occasional letter when he demeans himself by touting for work. One such letter to Dr James Taylor (1833–1900), organist of New College, Oxford, pleads "I must teach", yet ends with an extraordinary paragraph:

> If I can be of any use in offering remarks as to the accompaniment of the Choral services I shall be happy to hear you play. Excuse this offer as I have never had the pleasure Wherefore.

Another letter to the Precentor of Ely outlines a presumptuous plan where the small amount of money spent by cathedrals on new music should all be forwarded to him, for which he would produce a "new thing monthly". He continues:

> I do not think I have at the most, more than a few years left me, if that, but I should like to apply those years in the way I had meant my whole life to have been applied, that is, in composing.

A laudable idea, but one that he must have known would never be taken up.

He had by now established himself as a real 'character', possessing many eccentricities which included an obsession for fine clothes, many of which he never wore, and the collecting of curiosities, most of which piled up in spare rooms. He became a connoisseur of food and drink and enjoyed his garden. He also pursued his interests in the other arts, especially literature and painting. He rather enjoyed his reputation for being irritable and absent-minded. Yet he enjoyed a devoted following. He was well known in the city and especially around the cathedral precincts, often being seen in his favourite pose of pacing up and down dangling a glove by the finger-end, no doubt contemplating his next invective. He also frequently carried a huge umbrella, which elicited comments from acquaintances. On one occasion, having been asked the reason for its extravagant size, he is reputed to have said, "I am aware of it; you see it is going to have a lot of little parasols".

With his sons now educated it would appear that Samuel Sebastian was content to see out his time at Winchester, with the prospect of deriving increasing pleasure from leisure pursuits. The Dean and Chapter saw things differently. Wesley's constant disappearances from the Close with rod and line were becoming a serious embarrassment, especially as the deputies were often less than adequate, on one occasion a boy of fourteen. The Chapter minutes make frequent references to absences and sheer neglect of duty, and there are also instances of unpaid debts to the cathedral authorities, who on the whole showed remarkable tolerance. However it was almost inevitable that their patience would ultimately become exhausted and in 1865 he was requested to resign. Again he was in luck. John Amott (1798–1865), organist of Gloucester Cathedral had recently died and the Dean and Chapter there consulted Wesley on the appointment of his successor; to their surprise and delight he offered himself, an offer which was accepted gratefully. As a Canon of Gloucester remarked at the time, "it was as if the Archbishop of Canterbury had applied for a Minor Canonry". Wesley took up his appointment on 24th June, 1865, and was succeeded at Winchester by his pupil Dr George Arnold.

Gloucester

It is difficult to imagine that Wesley approached his work at Gloucester with any more relish than he had had for his previous appointments. Biographers have ranged in their assessments from "the happiest decade of his life", to "no happier than before" and "an unhappy end to a brilliant career". In view of the Doctor's capricious nature he no doubt expressed all three views during his time at Gloucester.

Although not an old man at the time of his appointment, he was not in good health and had become increasingly bitter. Having to lodge in the city, because the organist's house in Miller's Green was not ready for occupancy, caused him additional distress, contributing to the "pains all over" and "much debility", as expressed in a letter to his son Francis, who was still residing in Winchester. He had apparently aged considerably, looking older than his years, but his temper had not mellowed in any way. In an effort to involve him in local activities and make him feel welcome, Mrs Ellicott, the wife of the Bishop of Gloucester, had invited Wesley to meet and conduct a rehearsal of a Ladies' Society; after only a few minutes of hearing them sing he banged the lid of the piano and rushed from the room shouting, "Cats"! Hardly the behaviour to endear him to the 'county set'. Yet the Wesleys did enjoy a friendship with the Ellicotts, frequently turning to them for advice and support, including an unsuccessful attempt to start an organ rebuilding fund.

Wesley would have been relieved to find another appointment so easily in view of his tenuous position at Winchester, but if he had hoped for better things at Gloucester he was to be disappointed. The standards under his predecessor, Amott, had been mediocre, and every aspect of the music there had been allowed to deteriorate, including the organ, which was said to be in a poor state. The specification of the instrument that Wesley inherited is given in appendix ii, and readers will observe that there is little or no advance on the instrument that had given him so much pleasure at Leeds, and which had been so well maintained. The Gloucester organ had been rebuilt in 1847 by the young Henry Willis, who had considered it to be his "stepping stone to fame". By the time of Wesley's arrival this fine organ was in need of overhaul but, for once, he seemed to be prepared to live with the problems, for the organ was not to receive any further attention until 1888–89. At least Wesley had his organ on the screen and the console was on the east side, thereby providing the balance and liaison between accompanist and choir that he had been advocating so strongly. Not that the choir at Gloucester was particularly efficient; nor does it appear that Wesley had either the talent or the inclination to effect any improvement. There are many stories of his dealings with the choir and of his eccentric actions, even during some of the services. He was never content with the "modern tuning" of organs, even though mean temperament was clearly doomed, most organ builders having abandoned the old system in the rebuilds of cathedral and other important instruments that were sweeping the country. But he was still writing long letters to people on the subject. One such letter to Dr Ash, a friend from Holsworthy in Devon, stated:

> As to equal tuning — as you speak so clearly about it I will own I do not like it. It is a long story to enter on, so I will only say that I can never enjoy playing on an organ where nothing is in tune, where simple triads produce the effect on the ear which dissolving views do to the eye before the picture has reached its full focus. All the organ builders are against it, but have had to yield to fashion, and having once taken the plunge they are like the fox in the fable and recommend all foxes to give up their tails.

He goes on to suggest that the Germans were responsible for the new fashion, rebuking the conductor Sir Michael Costa (1808–84) for being ignorant on the matter. After some asides about "well-taught organists" and "good English conductors", which he clearly thought were in a minority, he ends:

> The old tuning has many friends and I don't hesitate to recommend it. But writers in the press may find fault with you if they know you don't adopt the fashionable practice. If nothing is said about it, they will not know anything.

He probably realised that he had lost this particular battle, but he was not likely to retract from his obsessions, on which he still expounded with great lucidity and strength. The tone of the above extracts are fairly predictable; another letter written at about the same time indicated more personal disappointments:

I ever regret leaving Devon, and Gloster [sic] is very objectionable. There is however no great demand for any peculiarly experienced musical ability and I must be content to rank with the low ones.

He had by then discovered that the Chapter at Gloucester were just as fickle as all the others. No doubt pleased to have secured the services of England's most renowned church musician at a time when mediocrity reigned supreme, they were nevertheless unco-operative and largely unconcerned. Wesley's reactions to this were not as dramatic as hitherto; nor did the Chapter react to his foibles as strongly as might have been anticipated, for there can be little doubt that — apart from his blatant flaunting of ecclesiastical decencies — he continued to take advantage of his deputies and remained guilty of unreasonable absences. After a short while Wesley lost interest in the choir completely, leaving their training in the hands of a lay clerk. History relates that at rehearsals the choir members made no attempt to sing, but merely whispered and hummed their parts. This tradition apparently continued for some time after Wesley's death.

There was less mention of fishing activities, although the rivers and streams of Gloucestershire and neighbouring Herefordshire would not have escaped his attentions. There is one story of Wesley, having been caught poaching and brought before the owner of the fishing rights, being recognised and asked to play and comment upon the new organ which had been installed in the house. Wesley obliged, afterwards sending a bill for ten guineas; the reply was an account for fifteen guineas for a day's fishing.

In spite of failing health he retained his love of the countryside, and he would have been delighted by his return to the Three Choirs territory for that reason alone. His life had become rather melancholy and he had even lost interest in his garden, which, according to Kendrick Pyne, became known locally as Wesley's Wilderness; but he was able to derive much solace from the companionship of his dogs.

He was able to sustain his interest in organ playing and, even though his abilities were declining and he complained of increasing lameness, he was much sought after as an organ recitalist, being especially associated with the opening of organs in cathedrals and churches, many of which had benefitted from his advice. One such recital was given at Worcester Cathedral in 1874 when he played the huge four manual organ of fifty-one speaking stops built by W. Hill and Son in the South Transept. At the restoration of Worcester Cathedral in the 1850s the organ had been removed from the central screen to the north side of the Quire, (a complete contradiction of Wesley's ideals). But it was found to be totally inadequate to the needs of any congregation in the Nave; hence the additional instrument in what proved to be a far-from-satisfactory site. The instrument, which was housed in a vast and ugly case designed by Sir Gilbert Scott (1811–88), was financed by the Earl of Dudley. This organ and the nobleman will appear later in the narrative. Wesley's superb playing on this occasion was to make a profound impression on one young member of the audience, Edward Elgar (1857–1934), who recalled that the recitalist "built up a wonderful climax of sound before crashing into the subject of the 'Wedge' Fugue of Bach". Elgar was not the only composer of the future to be thrilled by Wesley's playing. Hubert Parry (1848–1918), a member of an aristocratic family from Highnam Court near Gloucester, used to make frequent visits to the Cathedral there on his bicycle in order to hear Wesley play concluding voluntaries. Commenting on an extempore performance Parry wrote:

> He began the accompaniment in crotchets alone, and then gradually worked into quavers, then triplets and lastly semiquavers. It was quite marvellous. The powerful old subject came stalking in right and left with the running accompaniment wonderfully entwined with it — all in the style of old Bach.

There are many similar appreciations from people of lesser musical estimation, but all refer to the thrilling quality of his presentations.

It is surprising and disappointing that Wesley wrote little of importance while at Gloucester. He completed some straight-forward canticle settings which he had begun at Winchester, and wrote some small-scale anthems. *God be merciful unto us, The Lord is my shepherd*, and a group of short anthems written during his last years do not bear favourable comparison with his earlier works, as interesting as some of them are. There is a pleasing part song *When the pale moon* and an organ work, *Air with Variations: Holsworthy Church Bells*, presumably written in deference to his friend Dr Ash. Two *Andantes* and a *Voluntary* were discovered after his death, but no exact date can be ascribed to them. However, there is one work of real quality from his final years — *The Praise of Music* — an unaccompanied setting for eight voices of a poem by Thomas Oliphant (1799–1879), a fairly undistinguished Victorian poet best known for his English translations of Italian madrigals and songs. This short chorus of two sections recalls Wesley's old skills of manipulating choral counterpoint and sonorities, together with a natural gift of melody. This significant piece had been commissioned by Gounod for performance by his Royal Albert Hall Choir in 1872, another indication of the esteem in which Wesley's music was held by renowned European composers. Gounod described the work as a "beau morceau a huit voix"; he had previously told Wesley that he had formed a very high opinion of his compositions.

It may well be that the sparsity of compositions in the Gloucester period can be attributed to his commitment to the *European Psalmist*, a vast undertaking which he had been compiling for several years and which he was now under pressure to complete, not least because some of the original subscribers were departing this life at a worrying rate! He was still able to obtain in excess of five hundred names, including some of the country's leading musicians. The object was to collect as many hymn tunes as possible that had not been published in any other book, and which he had felt worth preserving. There are few examples from his own contemporaries, not surprising in view of the contempt that he had for most of the sentimental and inappropriate offerings, but he did contribute no less than one hundred and forty three of his own tunes, many of them among the finest in British hymnody. He also arranged and harmonised many others, especially those of German origin, including many from Bach. His devotion to the German tradition, especially post-Bach, was exploited to the detriment of much fine earlier English material. Allowing for the limitations imposed on the volume by his own restricted preferences, everything is tastefully presented — a production of real quality. There are 558 pages containing 733 items, 615 of which are hymn tunes. These are followed by settings of the Sanctus, single and double chants and short anthems. The book is completed by Samuel Sebastian's own *Chant Service in G*. This remarkable volume is the finest testament that any one individual ever made to hymnology.

In the thirty years following his departure from Hereford Wesley had made no contact with the Three Choirs Festival. He would find that little had changed. He had experienced one round of Festivals while at Hereford so the impending Gloucester Festival would have had few fears for him; certainly the Festival-goer would have been delighted to have the return of this distinguished musician in their midst, a musician now vastly more experienced. It must be assumed that his first programme in 1865 would have been chosen before he took up office, although he obviously had a hand in the choice of Service Music since no less than six of his pieces were designated to be sung by the Three Cathedral Choirs. The main programme would not have displeased him either, for it contained works by Handel, Mendelssohn, Mozart and Spohr. The extraordinary secular concerts that took place in outside halls during the evenings of the Festival contained an amazing variety of mostly trite pieces combined with operatic selections and the occasional larger work such as Mendelssohn's *First Walpurgis Night*, heard on this occasion. Wesley's own *Ascribe unto the Lord*, as previously orchestrated at Winchester, was included and much appreciated. In the same programme by special request "Dr Wesley played Bach's St Anne Fugue in his own admirable and original manner". It was documented that at this Festival "the performances were all that could be wished", an accolade for Wesley as a conductor who would have borne the brunt of the whole week's performances. Other references to his conducting skills are less reassuring. The *Musical Times* review of the 1865 Gloucester Festival said:

> We have said nothing of the orchestra during these performances, for in truth the perfect manner in which the whole of the instrumental portions of the works were performed left us with nothing to comment upon. The band . . . proved the very best friends of the conductor, a fact which he tacitly admitted by occasionally laying down his baton, and becoming an attentive and admiring conductor.

No doubt this was meant to be a tactful criticism of Wesley's reputation as a conductor who did not inspire confidence. There is one famous story of him falling asleep while conducting at a public concert, and another, as related in the *Musical Times*, of an incident in a rehearsal of an overture when

> . . . the band had played the final chord and yet the baton was still in action. The principal violin went up to the conductor and said: "We've finished, Doctor". "Finished", retorted Wesley, "why I have twelve more bars".

Wesley's first appearance at the Three Choirs Festival in 1834 had elicited no more than a passing comment in the Festival records that he was the conductor, but, as well as his Gloucester period being well reported, it was also a very significant time in the history of the Festival.

As was customary, at an 'away' Festival the visiting organists undertook the role of accompanist, either on the piano or the organ. Wesley did this with much distinction, although he created a stir when he refused to take part in the Worcester Festival of 1866. It is not known why, although it has been suggested that it was because none of his music had been selected; but he obviously sensed the mood of dismay that it created and never absented himself again. His music was usually represented at the Choral Services and at Hereford in 1867 he conducted again his "sublime anthem" *Ascribe unto the Lord*. It is interesting that his orchestrated *Wilderness* never appeared at these Festivals in his time. He seems to have behaved himself impeccably at 'away' Festivals, the only anecdote emanating from Hereford 1867 when he accompanied Miss Julia Elton at a secular concert.

> . . . as Miss Elton returned to the platform to acknowledge the applause the Doctor evidently thought than an encore was imminent, and accordingly took his seat at the piano and played the prelude to the song again, but the laughter of the audience convinced Dr Wesley that something was amiss, and on looking round he found that the vocalist had retired from the platform.

Wesley's Gloucester Festivals make interesting reading. The programme for the 1868 event was wider-ranging than any previous Festival including the inevitable Mendelssohn works, but also Handel's *Samson*, Spohr's *Calvary*, and a novelty by his father, *Confitebor tibi*. There were also two new works: a cantata by Joseph Schachner which "failed to make any great impression" and a "promising" new orchestral work, *Intermezzo Religioso* by the local composer, Hubert Parry. This more demanding programme for the chorus was to have disastrous consequences in the opening work of the Festival, Beethoven's *Mass in C* (called

Service in C in order not to offend low church sensibility). *The Annals of the Three Choirs* admit to "an unfortunate breakdown at the commencement of the *Kyrie*, owing to the uncertainty of the tempo adopted". It continues:

> . . . more disasters were in store, and by the time Miss Wynne came in with her solo hopeless confusion reigned supreme, so that the movement came to a sudden collapse, and was re-commenced.

The remainder of the Festival appeared to have proceeded without further mishap, other reports mentioning "the complete success of band and chorus under Dr Wesley's baton".

Massive repairs to the Quire of the Cathedral nearly prevented the 1871 Festival from taking place. The work was finished only shortly before the Festival began, and it was also noted that "the old cathedral organ was so flat that it was unusable with the orchestra". Another interesting fact is that Wesley's former pupil and assistant at Winchester, Kendrick Pyne, had now moved to Gloucester, where he played most successfully at the Opening Service of the Festival. The programme was again well-constructed with a judicious mixture of conventional oratorios and less-known works. Among the latter was Bach's *St Matthew Passion*, which Wesley introduced to the Festival audience for the first time. The performance was well received even though there had been several uneasy moments and the occasional breakdown. *The Times* was moved to say that

> The execution of this difficult music was, for the most part, excellent, allowing for a few uncertain moments, and Bach's 'Passion' will probably often be heard at the meeting of the Three Choirs. Where else can it be heard to such advantage?

The problem was that this mammoth work had been programmed with a new work by Sir William Cusins (1833–93) and selections from Spohr's *Calvary*, with the resulting effect that the end of the concert was performed to "a weary and vanishing audience". Although Wesley had again been criticised for his leisurely tempo during the week it is noted that at the final secular concert he was "received with cordial and prolonged applause on appearing to conduct a selection from *Figaro*".

During the time of Wesley's return to the Three Choirs scene there had been a growing feeling of uncertainty surrounding the future of the Festival. This was almost entirely due to the Cathedral authorities at Worcester who, encouraged by Lord Dudley, were "harbouring unfriendly intentions" towards the Festival on the grounds that it was becoming too secular. Lord Dudley, the benefactor of the organ previously mentioned, also attempted to blackmail the Chapter with offers of more financial support for the restoration of the building if they abandoned the Festival. The Chapter, to their credit, refused this offer, but still planned to reduce the 1875 Worcester Festival to a series of Services. The Gloucester Festival of the previous year took place under this shadow. Meetings of the Stewards were held and statements issued, all of which were to have no immediate effect on the decisions which had already been made at Worcester. Ironically the Gloucester committee had decided to replace the final night ball in favour of a Closing Service at which the preacher would be the Reverend Dr Barry, Canon of Worcester. The *Musical Times* reported that the reverend gentleman preached "a somewhat ominous sermon" after which, "as a practical comment on the tendency of that discourse, Dr Wesley played the Dead March in *Saul*"!

The Gloucester Festival in 1874 was full of interest. Wesley's personal interests were to the fore in the choice of works: Haydn's *Creation*, Mendelssohn's *Elijah* and *Hymn of Praise*, Spohr's *Last Judgement*, Rossini's *Solemn Mass* and *Stabat Mater*, Weber's *Praise of Jehovah*, and traditionally for the final concert Handel's *Messiah*, although with Mozart's orchestration. The secular concerts, now reduced to two, were as protracted as ever, but contained more refined music than usual, including some substantial items of Mozart. Two of Wesley's songs, *Silently, silently* and *The Butterfly* were sung by Miss Antionette Sterling; his music also appeared at all the Choral Services during the week. Wesley had asked Charles Gounod (1818–93) to write a work for the 1874 Festival, and the proposition looked hopeful; but, even though the composer had disclosed the title of the work, the plans never materialised, probably because everyone was preoccupied with the bad news coming down from Worcester. The concerts were well received although the chorus was judged to be unbalanced; but the poorest feature of the week was the bad singing of the Cathedral Choirs. One critic wrote that

60

> if the Service of that evening were to be taken as any specimen of
> what the future Festivals are to be, we tremble for the poor
> widows and orphans for whose benefit they are carried on, for
> assuredly more slovenly singing we have rarely heard within the
> walls of a Cathedral.

Hardly words of encouragement in view of the plans for the following year at Worcester, as well as being a sad reflection on the work of Wesley at the approaching end of a distinguished life.

The Worcester threats were duly carried out and the so-called 'Mock Festival' took place in August 1875. It was a non-event which brought credit to no one, except perhaps Samuel Sebastian Wesley, whose accompaniments and voluntaries on "The Earl of Dudley's Grand Organ in the South Transept" were the only redeeming features of this sad week. The local newspaper reported that "the immense capabilities of this monster instrument were well brought out by the Doctor". Elgar was again in attendance and once more voiced his enthusiasm for the manner of playing. He was also to experience at first hand Wesley's compositions, for several of the larger scale anthems and the *Service in E major* were sung during the week. The fine *Let us lift up our heart* must have made a good impression on Elgar, for he was to orchestrate it for a later Worcester Festival. This was be to Wesley's last appearance at the Festivals.

The Wesleys were now living quite comfortably. The music published by Novello was selling well and in 1873 he had accepted the then Prime Minister Gladstone's offer of a Civil List pension of £100 per annum, in recognition of his distinguished services to Church Music. He appreciated the honour, but he enjoyed more the "nice little nest egg", which would be continued to his widow. During his final years he kept the wheels moving at Gloucester, but very little more, and his health had now become a constant worry. He must have called on reserves of strength to fulfil his commitments to the Worcester Festival in 1875, for it had been a particularly bad year for him. Permanently on a weakening diet, he had become very depressed with his work and his house. "I don't like this place at all" he wrote to his sister. His last months must have been terrible indeed. Now known to be suffering from Bright's disease, a serious condition of the kidneys named after an early nineteenth century English physician, Richard Bright. This would have caused a loss of appetite and a severe disturbance of the digestive system, and probably swelling of the body. In addition he was also experiencing difficulty in breathing. He dragged himself to the Cathedral to play for the Christmas Services of 1875, his last service being Evensong on Christmas Day. Instead of playing his customary concluding voluntary of Bach, he asked his assistant for a full score of *The Messiah* which he kept in the organ; from it he played the *Hallelujah* chorus, much to everyone's surprise.

He never played the organ again and, after prolonged suffering, he died at his home on 19th April, 1876, at the age of sixty five. His last words were "Let me see the sky".

At his own request S.S. Wesley was buried in the family vault at the Old Cemetery at Exeter. Although the Cathedral authorities at Exeter chose to ignore the funeral, the choristers attended unofficially. His coffin was borne by four of his sons and he was laid to rest beside his baby daughter. His wife survived him by ten years. She died on 28th February, 1886, having moved to South Kensington after her husband's death.

Tributes were profuse and generous, none more so that that of the Prime Minister, who commented that he will be greater still in the eyes of those that come after. He is remembered in the form of stained glass windows or plaques in all the cathedrals that he served, together with Leeds Parish Church, and probably more has been written about him than any other church musician. The serious defects of his character were rightly overlooked as the ecclesiastical and musical world mourned the passing of a genius, the like of whom would be unlikely to grace their portals ever again.

2.

His Music

I t would be fair to say that, if confusion reigned over the English religious scene, a similar accusation could easily be levelled against English music, although apathy and self-satisfaction could be added to the collective ailments. For just over a century English music had been dominated by German infiltrators and generally the indigenous musicians had been happy to become mere imitators. The Handel domination had shown signs of waning at the beginning of the Victorian era, only to be replaced by the unbelievable charisma surrounding Mendelssohn, the most popular of a host of foreign musicians who regularly visited these shores, wielding enormous influence over their English counterparts; indeed, they were largely responsible for stifling the growth of national music here.

In all artistic pursuits, but most particularly in music, Britain was dominated by the Continent through most of the nineteenth century. The influences on music were varied: the ornate operatic traditions of Italian opera from Venice, the elegant offerings of that fun-loving city of Vienna, and the more serious instrumental styles of the Germans which, through the pens of Mendelssohn and his followers produced a bourgeois romanticism redolent of the age. Although Gounod was a frequent visitor to Britain, becoming a helpful friend to many musicians, including Samuel Sebastian Wesley, there was little interest in French culture. In any event the political and social climate of the time favoured the Teutonic way of life. The music of Venice and Vienna would decline quite dramatically during the century, which only served to strengthen the German hold and contribute still further to the insularity of home activities.

Instrumental styles, which had largely lain dormant in England since Purcell's time — with the notable exceptions of William

Boyce (1711–79) and Samuel Wesley — were still treated with much suspicion by our composers. George Hogarth, the father-in-law of Charles Dickens, writing in *Musical History, Biography and Criticism* in 1838, says:

> The composition of instrumental music either for a full orchestra or in the form of concerted pieces for instruments, has not yet been successfully cultivated in England. We have not symphonies, quartets or quintets which can rival the works of the German school.

Yet there were some essentially English cultures that demanded attention from our own musicians: the music for home entertainment with special emphasis on the new-found pleasures of the pianoforte, the lighter form of opera, and the revival of interest in the choral tradition.

Much of the music in the first category was rather feeble and certainly over-sentimental. Few composers contributed anything of real distinction, although viewed from a distance there is some music worthy of our attention; the writers were not without talent, but were writing for the demands of their time. The opera scene was more complex. Entirely dominated by Italian patterns, opera had for long been almost exclusively the domain of the aristocracy, the only 'local' attempts being little more than a medley of popular tunes with threadbare literary backing. There were some moves to improve the situation, led by the German-born Julius Benedict (1804–85), but the most significant advance was through the light operas of Sir Arthur Sullivan (1842–1901). His work is largely outside the period of S.S. Wesley, but the two composers are often linked as being pioneers in their own respective fields.

The interest in choral music in Britain was one area of cultural activity for which we did not have to show gratitude to the Germans, although this home-grown occupation was to have its repertoire enlarged, and in some instances enriched, by the copious continental contributions to the tradition. Mendelssohn had provided the pattern for oratorio, mainly through *Elijah*, his finest work in this genre, but he and his lesser German colleagues had also pointed the way with the shorter cantatas and part songs. The English part song, written for home and concert use, became very popular and there exist some fine examples of the form. It was inevitable that this type of composition would spill over into the realms of church music. It was not the first time that secular influences were absorbed into the church, and not only in music; nor will it be the last and, generally speaking, church music will benefit from it. Unfortunately the secular influences on church music of the nineteenth century were not always good; largely because of excessive sentimentality of both words and music, little of value emerged.

The fine balance between sentiment and emotion is ever present in church music. Controlled emotion is an essential part of worship, but so much church music produced before the emergence of S.S. Wesley lacked taste and was frankly banal. The better examples were those unpretentious small scale works that, in a sense, were natural sequels to the Viennese styles, as exemplified by Mozart's *Ave verum corpus*. Anyone attempting works on a larger canvas was less successful, producing note spinnings that were pale imitations of their continental benefactors. The Three Choirs Festival, and other choral festivals of the period, give a clear picture of the choral scene through their programmes. These were always dominated by Handel, Mendelssohn and Spohr, but there were usually 'novelties' by lesser composers, rarely British, on some obscure Biblical subject. Few of these works are worthy of serious consideration, a fact that was recognised even at that time, when appreciation was supposed to be at a low ebb. In view of his association with the Three Choirs Festival it is very surprising that Wesley did not exercise his gifts to produce a cantata or even an oratorio. He was the one composer of his time who could have achieved notable success in this field, and his reluctance to attempt anything larger than an orchestrated anthem remains a mystery.

The Nationalist movement, which was beginning to awake in eastern Europe, was not to reach fruition in Britain until nearly the twentieth century, although the Tractarians were to a certain extent responsible for revival of interest, not only in Tudor counterpoint and Plainsong, but also in folk music. As we have already seen, Wesley, in common with other notable musicians, was resistant to this revival of 'antique' cultures. They were well aware of the range of musical language available to them through the absorption of the modal harmony, but preferred to retain the trusted language of the German romantic school. For some forty or so years most 'modern' English music sounded like Mendelssohn! The confident new English voice was still a long way away, only to surface first with the work of Parry and Stanford and then, at the turn of the century, with the most powerful influence since Purcell, in the personage of Edward Elgar.

The advantage that Wesley had over his immediate contemporaries was that, in addition to the prevailing influences, he was also able to draw on the music of J.S. Bach, giving him an extra authority which the others could not begin to approach. Interestingly Stanford considered that Wesley was an important person in the "first fruits of the renaissance of English Music"; he also wrote that Wesley "had a genius for choral writing, and a grasp of new harmonic effects that were new to his day". In his *History of Music* (1916) he goes on to suggest that Wesley's cathedral music showed an independence of thought and mastery that was well above the heads of his listeners. Stanford continues that "he was little touched by the Mendelssohn fever, and preserved to the full the traditions of his own country". We may well argue with the former statement, but few would object to the remark that "he proved that the spirit of Henry Purcell was not dead in England".

From quite an early date musicians were acknowledging Wesley's importance in musical history. Certainly as far as church music was concerned he was considered to be the best composer since Purcell; some would even go so far as to say since Byrd. These are the traditions to which Stanford referred, not the musical language employed. In linking Wesley with Sullivan as shining examples of progress during a barren period in our musical history, we should remember that both men developed their art along very different lines. Both possessed genius and a freedom of expression that was largely allowed to develop without too close a watch on the prevailing styles and influences from the Continent, although a certain amount of these influences would unwittingly be absorbed into their compositions. It cannot be denied that both men made much use of music's commonplace materials, but perhaps there the comparison ceases, for Wesley was certainly more dexterous, especially in his richly sensitive harmonic style — a style that, when examined, proves to be distinctive and adventurous. Nor was he lacking special melodic gifts and lyrical appeal. Sullivan looked towards the Parisian scene for his melodic charm, but used the

German models for his harmony and construction; on the other hand Wesley was a more natural melodist, with a particular and recognisable turn of phrase, supported by a more complex harmonic language unashamedly developed from Spohr, his favourite composer. It must be said that Wesley's writing and intellectual word setting was far in advance of his contemporaries, carrying much more immediate influence than his original and considerable literary outpourings on the church and its music. It is interesting that no less a person than that most nationalist of composers, Ralph Vaughan Williams (1872–1958), in tracing the inheritance of English Music, makes a special mention of Wesley; this is not a random choice of name, but a citation of one whose mastery of musical language was capable of revealing new and exciting things. This Wesley certainly did, and the fact that he wrote almost to the exclusive benefit of the church in no way lessens his importance.

On the whole church music is inclineed to be less 'contemporary' than its secular counterparts and quite often, by the time that the new compositional techniques are used, the style has become overworked and outdated. We have certainly experienced this in recent years, to the detriment of positive progress in ecclesiastical music. Until quite late into our present century the liturgy had remained unchanged for a very long time, demanding a set pattern of composition; in addition so much of the repertoire was, and still is, drawn from the many styles, languages and cultures of the past. At the time of Wesley's entry into the profession the church itself had become moribund, so it was not surprising that, with the exception of the fine 'pure' works by his father and a handful of pieces by other composers, the familiar musical formulae required for the liturgy lacked imagination. But we should avoid being too critical of the men who composed these facile attempts to complement the worship. They were men of little distinction outside their organ lofts, and they were not writing for posterity. They were merely reflecting the kind of worship that they knew and presumably of which they approved. Sadly, this part of our unique heritage had become very parochial — a domestic affair that had little impact or significance on the wider sphere of cultural activity.

When Wesley graduated to the cathedral organ loft church music presented a depressing scenario. The services and the music designed for them had changed little since the seventeenth century, and the performances had fallen to a deplorable standard as a result of tedious repetition and lack of challenge. What would he be able to contribute to this decaying art that would be accepted, or even point a way forward? His response would be to ignore the current trends and to write from the heart, hopefully to influence, but also to write for the future well-being of cathedral music. With his ability and intellect he knew no other way. *The Wilderness* was his first major work, and it could not have been a more dramatic answer to the challenge. Few, except his closest admirers, could have anticipated the quality of his first serious undertaking and, although it has become fashionable to point out the weaknesses of the work, it still stands out like a beacon amidst the unctuous examples of work that surrounded it. Written in the same year as Newman's famous 'National Apostasy' sermon which heralded the Oxford Movement, Wesley's anthem is in its way just as significant.

The Wilderness was the first of Wesley's cantata-style anthems. He takes his text from the thirty-fifth chapter of Isaiah, interpreting it in a most original and personal way. There is no introduction, the bass solo immediately beginning the dialogue with one of the composer's trade marks — a melody based on the rising notes of a common chord, a feature that he was to use in many of his later works. The first movement is scored for a solo quartet in the manner of a rather superior part song, in which all the parts have lines of melodic interest. The second movement is allocated to a bass soloist, and it proves to be the finest section of the work. The English composers were not renowned for writing very distinguished tunes, but Wesley's solos were generally of a very different calibre from the trivial efforts found in other anthems of the time. *Say to them of a fearful heart* is a fine example of Wesley's art, with a strong and wide-ranging melody. After a short recitative for tenor, which could easily be mistaken for a passage from a baroque oratorio, the next section describing the "streams in the desert" contains more picturesque writing. The chorus briefly intercedes in a movement which is otherwise devoted to the solo quartet. Having changed colour through subtle, but favourite, modulations the movement reaches a dramatic climax in a phrase for the organ, before ending with some passages of choral recitative

— a device to be used with great effect in many of his anthems. The unexpected use of the high voices for "the redeemed shall walk there" is particularly effective. Then we realise why the chorus has been kept in reserve, for the brilliant penultimate movement is a vigorous choral affair in fugal form. It is in this type of movement that the influence of Bach is most strongly felt, giving this and other works moments of breadth that had been lacking for so long in cathedral music. Wesley said that "the 48 [Preludes and Fugues] contain all that is necessary for musical salvation" and that "the music of J.S. Bach is the Alpha and Omega of the Art". This strong belief was to be a great asset to him in his compositions. Yet Bach cannot claim credit for the stunning end to this fugue: having expressed the word "joy" by several lines of continuous quaver movement for the voices, the final peroration is anything but predictable as the music moves through a series of amazingly bold modulations. This is originality of the highest order. The reaction to all this exhuberance is a final movement of beautiful melodic flow, which obviously pays homage to the chromatic language of Spohr. Sentimental it may be, but few would be prepared to deny its moving effect when sung well — and it is difficult, not least because of the cruel tessitura for the treble soloist. The other, and perhaps most important feature of this elegant work is the independent organ part, written out on three staves and with copious directions for registration clearly designated by the composer. He obviously took special delight in the free-speaking pedal department of his new Hereford organ by writing some extremely awkward accompaniments, especially for the bass aria. He rarely took so much care with his accompaniments in the future; perhaps he felt that his colleagues would be incapable of playing them. He would probably have been correct in such an assumption.

The other important Hereford anthem, *Blessed be the God and Father*, has a tighter construction, the five concise movements being linked without a break. Considering the conditions affecting its composition and subsequent first performance it remains a striking work. The opening is magical. Beginning unaccompanied was a bold enough move, but reserving the organ for the final bars of the section to emphasise the words "the resurrection of Jesus Christ from the dead" may well have been considered foolhardy at the time, and indeed continues to cause tremors of excitement even

in present-day performances. But there is no denying the effect-
iveness of the idea. The second and fourth sections of the anthem
are devoted to choral recitatives assigned to the unison voices of
alto, tenor and bass. Wesley clearly enjoyed the sound of the alto
voice at its lowest extremities, for he habitually writes for them in
this way, but in the modern choir it would be a rare alto who would
relish singing these passages at pitch. I inherited an interesting
manner of performance at Leeds Parish Church for these passages,
where the altos sang the melody an octave higher than the tenors
and basses, claiming that it was the way that had been handed down
from Wesley. I found it difficult to believe, and anyway it sounded
eccentric, but it was a fascinating theory. These two recitative
sections have excellent declamation and provide the contrast of
colour and key that the anthem needs to avoid monotony of
tonality. The central section, a conversation for solo and chorus
trebles, has all the melodic charm of a Mendelssohn song, and is
none the worse for that. It is this part of the anthem, more than any
other, that has endeared it to singers and congregations of several
generations. After the second chromatic recitative where the voices
sink to their lowest note for "falleth away" there follows the famous
chord. How Wesley must have relished making everyone jump at
that point! But this is no joke; it is the sort of device that we
normally associate only with the great designs of Beethoven — a
simple over-used romantic chord, but never used in such a
dramatic way before. Nor could it ever be used in this way again;
Wesley has the copyright for all time. The chord ushers in a short
exuberant movement which makes concessions to counterpoint,
but which never really builds upon the power of the opening
antiphonal interplay between choir, using the rising arpeggio figure
to great effect, and the full organ. Again the organ part is important,
although not as enterprising as in *The Wilderness*, but another
notable feature here is the choice of the words and their impeccable
setting. Unlike his forbears and contemporaries Wesley was not
prepared to rely solely on the Psalms for his texts; he preferred to
choose widely from the Bible, with which he was very familiar,
sometimes selecting verses from different parts of the Book. He also
used parts of the liturgy and Prayer Book translations of psalms,
and was even prepared to incorporate metrical psalms if it suited
his purpose to stress a point. He chose verses from the First Epistle

of Peter for his Easter anthem, and it is doubtful that they will ever receive a better setting. These two Hereford anthems also emphasised his preference for keys lying between E flat and G; he rarely strayed from this area of tonality for choral music.

Wesley's next large scale anthem was *O Lord, thou art my God*, his doctorate exercise. This was his longest work in any form. Its length is probably the reason for its neglect, although one movement from it — *For this mortal must put on immortality* — has been regularly used as a separate anthem. Wesley himself extracted movements from his longer pieces to use as separate anthems, so establishing a precedent for this practice. Actually this movement, which has become the most familiar part of the anthem, is probably the weakest, although its jaunty rhythm and approachable tunes are attractive enough and, in the context of the complete work, afford effective and necessary contrast to the severity of the contrapuntal writing in the supporting movements, which are almost symphonic in proportion. The anthem, which draws its text from a remarkable collage of Biblical sources ranging from the Psalms, through Isaiah and the Wisdom of Solomon to extracts from the fifteenth chapter of the first book of Corinthians, has the longest introduction of all Wesley's anthems. It introduces some ingenious writing for double choir, which shows greater allegiance to Bach than any other anthem that he wrote. This work may well have been modelled on the double choir Motets of the earlier master. The words are beautifully expressed and there are again some daring modulations; but the finest feature of the whole anthem is in the polished part writing. The second movement is another aria for bass, although this one is of only moderate interest. This is followed by a rather four-square double chorus at the end of which the sudden introduction of rapid movement into the organ part only seems to emphasise the vapidity of the writing at this point. As already mentioned the fourth choral movement provides a pleasing enough interlude, but the final part of the anthem is very impressive. Beginning in eight parts, but eventually settling into five, this long movement is an amazing example of Wesley's skill in counterpoint. It is an academic construction, but emotion and colour are not excluded from this extraordinary movement, written in the grand style. In spite of some routine passages, it is not difficult to understand Dr Crotch's ready acceptance of the work for Wesley's doctorate. He would not have had many works of this stature submitted for the highest degree during his tenure of office at Oxford.

A work of comparable length, but arguably of greater interest is *Let us lift up our heart*. The date of composition is unknown, but its style and assurance would seem to place it in the Leeds or early Winchester period. The choice of texts for this anthem is even more interesting, ranging from the Lamentations of Jeremiah, the Psalms and Isaiah to verses of Charles Wesley. This monumental work in five sections is notable for its rare integrity and, even for Wesley, an exceptional sensitivity to the words, which were apparently chosen while he was composing the anthem. In this way he could shape the work to his own liking and not be restricted in any way by a predetermined text. The result is an anthem containing moments of high inspiration. It begins with a double chorus of passionate intensity and some especially effective antiphonal writing, but these sonorities are abandoned half way through the movement in favour of more conventional four-part writing, albeit with some beautifully wrought counterpoint. This leads directly into a more homophonic verse section for four voices which, although it lacks the inspiration of the remainder of the anthem, never sinks to vulgarity — Wesley never does. But the gem of the work is the wonderful bass aria that constitutes the third movement. Wesley never wrote a better piece than this, the lovely sweep of melody pervading the whole aria in its expression of the spirit of prayer. The first edition of the anthem clearly states that this should be sung by a bass, and it is a pity that later editions offer a contralto alternative, for this would surely rob this masculine solo of its dignity. As always in his arias there is an imaginative organ accompaniment; what a pity that he did not provide similarly interesting accompaniments for the remaining choral sections of the anthem; or perhaps his choirs demanded a more solid backing! This noble anthem ends with a strong and melodious chorale-like section and a subdued fugal chorus, leading to a characteristically quiet ending. This is cultured and devotional music; Wesley in his most original and distinctive style. No one else could have written this anthem; it is essential to know it if Wesley's art is to be understood. Elgar knew it and loved it well enough to respond warmly to Sir Ivor Atkins' invitation to orchestrate the anthem for performance at the Worcester Festival of 1923.

The two other important cantata anthems come from the Winchester period. *Ascribe unto the Lord* is an understandable favourite with choirs. Although on a large scale the individual movements are more concise than the previous anthems we have been considering, having a lot of variety and immediate attraction. The work commences with a massive unison song for the men's voices — the distinctive touch which we have already encountered in *Blessed be the God and Father* — but, just as impressive are the two full choir interjections to the words "Let the whole earth stand in awe of him": the first depicting tremendous strength and adoration, the second portraying hushed wonder before the presence of God. The cheerful quartet for two trebles and two altos that follows has a sort of eighteenth century elegance not often hinted at in Wesley's sacred works. This quartet also gives an idea of the technique and range of voice that he expected from his soloists. The short fugal chorus "As for the gods of the heathen" is in a mocking spirit and, with its chromaticisms and crisp rhythms, is reminiscent of a crowd scene from one of the Passions. At this point Wesley changes his text from Psalm 96 to Psalm 115, and the three short sections that continue the anthem — Recitative, Verse and Chorale — produce some unexpectedly trite writing; but the final chorus, often sung as a separate anthem, (*The Lord hath been mindful*), is magnificent in its grace and easy-flowing lines. The general theme of the anthem is praise of God and condemnation of idolatry: the composer expresses both with sympathy and understanding.

Praise the Lord, O my soul is another charming anthem. As previously mentioned it was written for the occasion of an organ opening at a city church in Winchester. The organ part itself is not particularly adventurous, except for a couple of passages that rush about rather aimlessly on the manuals, presumably to show to advantage the quick-speaking flue work on the new instrument. On the other hand the choral writing is first class, indicating a most proficient choir at the church. All the composer's characteristics are evident throughout: the unison passages for men, the wide-ranging solo lines, the subtle and sparing use of chorus, the exceptionally low line for the altos, and the beautiful tensions and sonorities evolved from a brilliant use of expressive suspensions and discords that are diatonic (i.e. the notes of the prevailing major or minor key — the opposite of chromatic). There are other noteworthy features in this anthem. The treble is the leading soloist, and he is allocated a beautiful line, rivalling the better-known example of an anthem by Mendelssohn for sheer fault-lessness of writing for this unique voice. There is also a feeling of unity not always apparent in his anthems, created here by the reappearance of leading tunes and by a carefully designed sequence of keys and modulations. As the end of the anthem approaches there is an inevitable chorale section which has a certain grandeur, especially if it is not taken too fast; but the actual final section is a gem. So simple, direct and sincere, it is not hard to understand why *Lead me, Lord* has become such a 'popular' piece of church music. The text is taken from Psalms 103 and 3, but the sequence of selected verses is another indication of Wesley's literary responses as well as his knowledge and understanding of theology.

All of the anthems discussed thus far were obviously modelled on the lengthy verse anthems of the previous century, works with which Wesley would have been very conversant, as they were the standard fare of cathedral choirs. 'Verse' is the term used in English church music to denote a passage or movement for solo voices, often a trio or quartet, as contrasted with the full choir, hence 'Verse' Anthem. Apart from the more advanced harmonic language, Wesley's works show a remarkable improvement on the earlier verse anthems because of their greater depth of feeling, their felicitous word setting, and their vastly superior melodic invention. All of these anthems are remarkably different and all are inventive, over-long though some of them may be.

Falling midway between the cantata and motet-type anthems are two interesting three-movement works. The familiar *O give thanks unto the Lord* is not one of Wesley's most inspired efforts, not least because he finds it difficult to give sufficient contrast, all the movements being firmly settled into the same key. Beginning with two of his favourite devices, a men's chorus singing the rising arpeggio tune, the first chorus is completed by a rather academic fugue, the subject of which has affinity with the attractive, mellifluous aria for treble solo (although very effective when sung by a chorus of trebles) which occupies the central position of the anthem. The usual reflective ending, two long phrases of quartet answered by the chorus, provides a fitting contrast, without ever capturing the spirit of *Lead me, Lord.* Much less known is *The face of the Lord,* also undated but, because of its similarity to the mood of *Cast me not away,* it might well have come from his time at Leeds. This is a good piece and its almost total neglect is puzzling. The first movement, scored for five voices, making use of two tenors, has some intensely expressive moments without resorting to excessive chromaticisms to make its point, and there is an arresting passage for unison (everyone singing the same tune) men's voices, with sonorous accompaniment making use of the G pedal-board, to the words "But the Lord delivereth him out of all". The middle section is the responsibility of a double quartet of soloists, singing in combination and antiphonally, that is two groups of singers stationed apart singing alternately — one of the oldest devices known to church music. There are some particularly interesting effects in this verse section, especially the heartfelt accents that are accorded to the word "cry". The full choir return for the last movement, which is disappointingly short and rather formal.

The first movement of this noteworthy anthem also shows another side to Wesley's compositional techniques. We tend to think that he had a rather grumpy view of the older composers and their adherence to the ancient modes, but here his writing is tantalisingly close to their techniques. Later in the movement he also has a juxtaposition of remote keys and progressions that few had dared to experiment with since Bach, an effect which heightens the words "broken heart" and "contrite spirit"; this is indeed bold writing, and it is this sort of thing which stands him apart from his contemporaries and makes him such an important influence on the English renaissance composers who were to follow some thirty years later.

Cast me not away, his undisputed masterpiece, is in the same mould as well as being in the same key as *The face of the Lord,* with similar sonorities and use of tonal contrasts by careful placing of groups of voices. This setting of verses from Psalm 51 for six voices is worthy to rank with the best church music produced of any age. The vocal lines flow and interweave in a manner that we would normally associate with the greatest of the Elizabethan composers, and it is only towards the end that a more 'modern' mode of artistic expression is used to give a rather sardonic interpretation to "that the bones which thou hast broken may rejoice" — a pertinent reminder of his fishing accident. This makes a good legend, but it should not disguise the fact that this is a magnificent anthem, which incidentally sounds well unaccompanied. The exceptional beauty of the final bars should be noted too. I well remember Herbert Howells (1892—1983) extolling the virtues of the final cadence, and he knew well how to manipulate a cadence himself. Howells is of course in direct line with Wesley, through Stanford, and his contribution to cathedral music in this century is as significant as Wesley's was in the last.

Of almost the same quality of *Cast me not away* is the much-loved *Thou wilt keep him in perfect peace*, which has been described by Eric Routley, a recent biographer of the Wesley family, as being "an almost perfect cathedral sound". Wesley knew when he had written a good tune, and he wrote none better than the memorable opening phrase for trebles, supported by sensitive lines for the four lower voices (again he writes for two tenors) and organ. There is another interesting collocation of texts, this time from Isaiah, the first epistle of John and a couple of isolated verses from the Psalms. The result is that he is able to manipulate his texts to create a 'rondo-type' anthem in which the opening melody can be heard three times. Another moving cadence makes use of the much-used cliché of earlier composers — the flattened seventh degree of the scale; but it was never before used more effectively than this.

The third of the shorter, one-movement anthems which still maintains its popularity in cathedral repertoires is the romantic *Wash me throughly from my wickedness*, the text taken from the same Psalm that inspired his finest work. This penitential anthem with its arresting opening melody for treble solo has a poignancy and dignity of expression that successfully avoids the stigma of sentimentality, and certainly doesn't deserve the harsh criticism levelled against it by some writers. The sort of criticism which dismisses the anthem as worthless because one note of the famous chord which supports the word "throughly" in the second bar fails to resolve according to the text books shows very little understanding of Wesley's skills. The last page of the anthem with its slow progression of common chords and an elongated 'English ending' does look drab on paper, but can be transformed when sung well and with sustained tone; here he makes his most effective and subdued use of his favourite 'rising chord motive'.

Most of the remaining anthems, apart from the early experimental pieces which do not really command our attention, generally follow the patterns of the works which we have been considering. He wrote no other true cantata anthems, but some, such as *God be merciful unto us* (Psalm 67) and *The Lord is my shepherd* (Psalm 23), are in several short sections, making use of solo voices or quartets to qualify them as verse anthems; but apart from using the Wesley hallmarks and having pleasing tunes, they have little distinction and are not often heard these days. Yet it is interesting that when Stanford wrote his own setting of the twenty-third Psalm only ten years after Wesley's he chose the same key and the same pattern of movements. This was probably no coincidence for he would have almost certainly known Wesley's later works. Herbert Howells, one of Stanford's many famous pupils, described this work as "one of the supremely lovely anthems in all our history", but he was equally enthusiastic of Wesley's setting which, together with many other works, he would have experienced at first hand during his student days in the organ loft at Gloucester. I remember being impressed with these lesser-known Wesley works myself when, as a chorister and later as assistant at Gloucester, I either sang or played them. Their recent neglect may well be unjust; perhaps we should blow the dust off the boxes and try them again.

We must assume that one of the reasons for Wesley turning to smaller scale anthems would have been the disappointment at the infrequency of performance of his 'grander' works; yet so often in his later works of the Gloucester period he is guilty of purveying platitudinous occasional pieces such as *Let us now praise famous men*. Had he only left us works of this nature history would have parcelled him up with all the other composers of little consequence. Undoubtedly his 1853 collection of anthems must be considered to be his best, but it would be wrong to overlook some of the others that were not included or were written later. These include a beautiful miniature *I am thine, O save me*, which first appeared in March 1857 as a supplement to the first issue of *The Musical Remembrancer*, a monthly magazine which enjoyed only a short life. The composer later revised the anthem, dedicating it to his friend

Dr Linnington Ash of Holsworthy. The revisions included rewriting some of the inner parts and adding an organ part for a few bars towards the end, which had originally been left unaccompanied. He leaves the voices unsupported on so few occasions in his music so we must assume that the ever-present accompaniment is an indication of his frustration at the inefficiency of his choral singers. This little anthem has many of the qualities of *Thou wilt keep him*, and the composer can be relied upon not to miss an opportunity of giving expressive treatment to such words as "perished" and "trouble". Another most interesting work is the setting of a paraphrase of verses from Psalm 119, *To my request and earnest cry*. The style is unmistakable: shapely melodic lines, enhanced by rich harmonies of a more chromatic nature than his later works employ, and a slow-moving summing-up at the end. The accompaniment is rather more independent than usual and the general feeling of the piece suggests that it might well have been originally designed as the first movement of an abandoned cantata anthem. It was found in a manuscript volume in the library of Leeds Parish Church by Sir Edward Bairstow (1874–1946), one of Wesley's successors at Leeds, who subsequently published the anthem in 1906. It should be heard more; it has all the devotional qualities of the composer's deeply felt works. Even in an anthem which he had either forgotten or discarded we see again the skilful handling of voices in full harmony to produce some profundly beautiful effects. Bairstow had also been responsible for revival of interest in *Let us lift up our heart*, which he meticulously edited for publication in 1914.

Two of the shorter anthems from the Collected Edition are *O Lord my God* (subtitled 'Solomon's Prayer') and the Funeral Anthem *Man that is born of a woman*. The first is of only passing interest, but does have an alternative final three bars of high notes to be substituted if "the treble part be sung by females", rather suggesting a lack of confidence in the ability of his trebles to sing with 'head' voice. The latter anthem is dignified and moving in its intensity, as befits its designated use. Great pathos is portrayed at "bitter pains of death", but the influence here is obviously Purcell; indeed Wesley intended that Purcell's *Thou knowest Lord* should be sung immediately afterwards. Wesley's other funeral anthem *All go unto one place* has been confused by historians with a setting of the same words by Samuel senior. There is no comparison between the two settings. The former is academic and chorally dull, the latter another example of the younger composer's adept grasp of setting sensitive and penitential texts. The two movements are in expressive block harmony, although there is an effective departure from this when the words "And now, Lord, what is my hope?" are sung in unison as a refrain. This impressive work has some relationship to *Let us lift up our heart*, and is only marred by a feeble and inappropriate organ link between the movements. Why did he do his sort of thing?

If Wesley had written none of these anthems we should still have been grateful to him for his stupendous *Service in E major*. This is indeed his magnum opus. By the time of the composition of these canticles Wesley had become the assured composer; he knew what he wanted and he knew how to achieve it, and it would have done no harm at all to his grand design for these works to know that his choir at Leeds Parish Church would be able to sing them. We now regard this Service to be the composer's most important contribution to the corpus of Cathedral Music, and in its time it was as significant and influential as the Great Services of Byrd and Tomkins. He showed that there was still something to be found for inspiration from these familiar texts; his settings are always imaginative and at times exciting; they are conceived in the grand manner in one of his preferred keys. He clearly considers that the liturgical requirements of the canticles suggest a fairly continuous passage of text, even if he occasionally indulges in repetition to stress a particular theological, or perhaps more often a musical point. The structure may not be very taut at times, but he regularly gives expression to the words by subtle variations of voice groups and the most colourful modulations. Another Wesley device used more frequently in these settings than elsewhere is the use of an arresting chord, or series of chords, to emphasise a word or crucial change of mood, that he is not able to dwell upon in any other way.

The *Te Deum* is a remarkably concise setting. Beginning in ceremonial style, the first phrase alone generates excitement as it rises over a held bass note to the highest note of the canticle; Wesley leaves little doubt that this is truly a song of praise. All the familiar devices are here, including some of his most effective unison passages for the men. There are some glorious modulations, mostly following his favoured formulae, but there is virtually no counter-point. One of his loveliest pieces of writing anywhere occurs at "O Lord, save thy people", where the feeling is enhanced by a rare excursion into the warm, but remote, key of A flat. This period of serenity is continued by a treble soloist, as the music gradually works back to the mood and the music of the opening, thereby giving this notoriously difficult canticle a sense of unity. The *Jubilate Deo* is even finer, with a splendour approaching the opulent Venetian motets, especially in the *Gloria*, which seems to reflect Wesley's appreciation of some of the works of Gabrieli. There has always been some hesitation on the interpretation of the section "and come before his presence with a song" for Wesley's note values appear to be ambiguous. Most performers are now prepared to accept the suggestions in the edition prepared by his pupil and assistant at Winchester, George Garrett, who explained that "he [Wesley] intended to express in his music the difference between a song of praise and an act of devotion". Earlier in his preface to the revised edition of 1896 Garrett throws some interesting light on Wesley's careless presentation of his scores and his reputed indecision on matters of interpretation:

> It has been by no means an easy task to edit this Service. Revision was made necessary in every page, I had almost said in every bar, by reason of Wesley's extraordinary carelessness in writing; and his meaning was often (partly from the same reason) so obscure, that only my recollection of his own treatment has enabled me to give any indication of it.

A typical bass solo of wide range and an eight-part verse section are pleasing moments in this canticle setting, but at the start of the *Gloria* he achieves one of his most startling effects — a fairly innocuous interlude on the organ being amazingly transformed by the full choir's entry on the unlikely chord of D sharp major. This would have played havoc with his mean temperament! What follows is also fairly remarkable — a durchkomponiert (through-composed, or fully worked out) setting of the remaining verses. The choir, now in eight parts, moves through all manner of keys and musical devices, all of which serve to gather up excitement for the impressive solemnity of the final Amens. Many of the ideas and key schemes of these canticles had been tried before in *The Wilderness*, but the writing in this *Gloria* transcends all that had

1. Samuel Sebastian Wesley at 25

2. Samuel Wesley, composer, father

3. Charles Wesley, evangelist, grandfather

4. The organ at Leeds Parish Church, with its controversial case

5. Portrait of Wesley held at Gloucester Cathedral

6. The first page of Wesley's anthem, 'Blessed be the God and Father', from the first printed edition of *Twelve Anthems*

7. The first page of 'Cast Me Not Away'

8. Line drawing of Wesley, date unknown

9. The memorial plaque to Wesley at Leeds Parish Church, unveiled in 1907

been achieved hitherto. What a shock these morning canticles would have been to the congregations brought up on the meagre fare of unadventurous 'short' settings of the canticles. Wesley made it known how much he despised these dreary settings; his answer to them was certainly startling. The transformation was too sudden. The church was not ready for such radical musical changes. As a result the *Service in E major* was little used in Wesley's lifetime, except at Leeds Parish Church, where they were "proud" to sing the Doctor's works.

For the Communion Service Wesley sets the *Responses to the Commandments*, a *Sanctus* and the *Nicene Creed*, which contains some interesting features. The middle section again uses the flat key of the *Te Deum* for a treble solo at "who for us men", although Wesley did sketch in a supporting role for the men's voices; there is also a flowing organ part at this point which sounds strangely out of place. The unison voices climbing up a chromatic scale at "and the third day he rose again" against a constantly moving organ part is effective, as is the reprise of the opening material for "he shall come again", but the final section of the *Creed* is given over to measured chanting — as unexpected as it is convincing.

The 1896 edition incorporates a much earlier setting of a *Gloria in Excelsis*. This is a dull affair which looks, and sounds, terribly out of place in its distinguished company.

The *Magnificat* and *Nunc Dimittis* continue the exalted mood of the Morning Canticles. All the distinctive features of Wesley's style are apparent on almost every page, especially in the *Magnificat*, where the juxtaposition of keys are as effective as anywhere in his compositions. Notable points are the double verse at "And his mercy", the warmth of tone created by the double chorus at "Abraham and his seed", and the radiance imparted to the music on the rare occasions when he uses a 'flat' tonality. The *Nunc Dimittis* has a more sombre tone, but is no less inventive, the ending of the canticle proving to be particularly exciting as it prepares for the unique and powerful entry of the *Gloria*, borrowed from the *Jubilate*, although here much shortened. The composer himself suggested that the *Gloria* could be "substituted for the one to the *Jubilate*, should the latter be found too long for use at Morning Service".

It is unfortunate that for over a hundred years editors both in and out of print have endeavoured to 'improve' Wesley's score of this Service. It may be true that the organ parts are not laid out for comfortable use on modern instruments and that the voice parts are used to their extremities, which contemporary musicians feel makes for a poor balance, but few, if any, of these alterations are justified. These same editors would take a poor view of those who would tamper with the great works of the sixteenth and seventeenth century; why should Wesley be treated differently? He may have been careless, but he was not incompetent. It is a measure of the greatness of his music that he can take all this meddling and still come out of it with distinction. The monumental *Service in E major* became the model for all the best canticle settings which followed later in the century, and indeed beyond it, for certainly there are several Evening Canticles sung regularly from Edwardian and later composers that have a distinctive Wesley flavour, and I find that even Elgar's *Te Deum* and *Benedictus*, written in 1897, show strong influences of the earlier composer.

The elaborate settings of canticles would eventually become accepted but, at the time of the *Service in E*, the 'short' services continued their dismal way. Even though Wesley had written and said some disparaging things about them and their composers he did feel moved to write one of his own — in the key of F. Wesley in F is not particularly original, although it does give some evidence of having been written by a composer of stature, without ever escaping from the traps of triviality, of which he was quick to accuse his fellow composers. He said that this Service and his other 'Chant' Services for parish use were attempts "to attain the utmost brevity without sacrificing expression in setting the Te Deum, etc. to Music".

Wesley's other choral works are not of great importance. His early experimental works for the church have fallen into oblivion and any revival would detract from the excellence of the accepted repertoire of services and anthems. The same is true of the secular pieces. At their best the part songs are pleasing enough, but add little to what was already known of this nineteenth century art form in Britain. Wesley's efforts compare favourably with the likes of Barnby, Bishop, Pearsall and others of that ilk, but no more. He certainly didn't follow his father's lead in this particular field, as the glees and part songs of the elder Wesley are mostly very fine, following in the traditions of the English madrigalists. One notable exception was the *Ode: The Praise of Music*. This two movement piece for double choir is written in a rococo style that would not be instantly recognisable as having been written by the composer of *The Wilderness* or the *Service in E*, but it has good tunes and some spacious harmony; it would have given great delight to Gounod's Albert Hall Choir, the forerunner of the Royal Choral Society.

Wesley wrote songs, many of them to sacred texts, through most of his life. Like the part songs they say little that is new. The melodic lines are pleasant and, as we would expect, careful attention is generally given to accentuation and appropriate word underlay, but the end products are no better than the well-known ballads of Balfe, Benedict and Sullivan. They suffer from similar ills of repetition, lack of colour (his skills of modulation rarely appear in these slighter musical forms), poor lyrics and rather routine accompaniments. He wrote little piano music and, what there is, coupled with the song accompaniments, rather suggest that he was not particularly enamoured with the instrument. However, the organ is a different proposition. Here the composer was on much safer ground, even if his compositions for the instrument appeared at spasmodic intervals and, on the whole, fail to sustain the high level of invention that we have come to expect from the anthems. We have previously discussed the nature of the English organ at the time of S.S. Wesley, and have perceived the restrictions imposed by most instruments. It follows then that the works written by Wesley would have taken these problems into account. His organ works were for the most part written on two staves for instruments with a G pedal-board and interest almost exclusively confined to the manuals, with much of the writing being thoroughly pianistic. The works themselves are fairly rhapsodic, being suggestive of an extempore exercise rather than in any serious formal instrumental style. Brilliant extemporisers often find it difficult to transfer their skills to the manuscript paper.

The best-known organ work is the *Choral Song*, often given the incorrect title of *Choral Song and Fugue*. The first section is a solid march-like movement with enough strength to make it suitable for a ceremonial occasion; the second movement, beginning as a sort of fugue, has for its subject a tune which resembles almost exactly the theme of a duet from John Travers' anthem *Ascribe unto the Lord*, a work which would have been in the repertoire of Wesley's choirs. The idea of the movement being a well-wrought fugue is soon abandoned and the remainder of the piece is really like a lively two-part invention, with increased 'padding' as the music works towards its final peroration. The 'fugue' may not have much substance, but it is enjoyable to play and has several humorous touches. There is not so much of Wesley's music in such a cheerful vein that we can afford to ignore this 'smiling' work. The *Larghetto* is also quite familiar. A pleasant minor key melody of some length which introduces the work is immediately worked into a variation in which the player's right hand — and the flute stops — are given a demanding test of repetition and agility. Then, almost as if the composer had lost interest, instead of continuing the variation potential, there is a very ordinary middle section before the principal tune is brought back abruptly to end the work in a slightly frustrating manner. It is not the only instance of Wesley bringing back the main theme at what feels to be too soon — *Thou wilt keep him* is another example.

Variation form was popular with the listening public and Wesley had indulged quite successfully in the form for his early organ work *Variations on the National Anthem*. No one would seriously consider writing a set of variations on the Anthem these days (although the American, Charles Ives, has done so on the same melody, which he calls *America*!), either because the tune doesn't excite them or because they would have more respect for the monarch. Wesley would not have had the same worries for, at the time of his Variations, the association was not as sacrosanct. It is just as well, for the work is delightfully vulgar! It expresses the enthusiasm of youth, together with the obvious pleasure that the young Wesley would have derived from displaying his own technical skills through this 'flashy' work. It enjoyed popularity for a long time, even being published in a *Coronation Album* in 1901. His famous extemporisations which excited so much favourable comment were in themselves a type of variation form but, apart from the fairly inconsequential variants on an air by the eighteenth century Viennese composer, Leopold Kozeluch in 1830, he didn't return to this form again until the last years of his life, when he wrote *Air with Variations: Holsworthy Church Bells*, a work which is fairly lightweight and, like the *Ode: The Praise of Music* written at about the same time, seeks a simpler, easier style.

The two undated *Andantes* are effective pieces in the Mendelssohn style. Obviously written for the prevailing mood of sentiment they are nevertheless discreet and tasteful. The *Andante in G*, the more substantial of the two, was actually laid out on four staves, making it very complicated to read — an indication of the composer's own dexterity and large hands, although, typically, he used to complain that his stretch was restricted. This is just as apparent in his finest work for the organ, the *Introduction and Fugue in C sharp minor*, where some extremely awkward stretches are called for. This work, which comes from the composer's most formative years, finds him in a serious mood. The introduction is short, but powerful, and provides the material for the fugue that follows. A fugue is one of the most revered forms of musical composition, and the ability to write one is regarded as possessing suitable academic status. The form itself is a type of contrapuntal composition in which a number of parts (or voices) enter successively in imitation with a theme which is known as the subject. There are innumerable rules governing this complex musical form, together with a host of musical devices which can be used. A good fugal work-out is no mere mathematical puzzle, but a creation of much emotion, even if the established composers bend the rules to achieve it. Wesley inherited his skill at fugal invention from his father and also from his keen study of the works of that master of fugue, J.S. Bach. His choral fugues are mostly satisfying, even if he has a reluctance to commit the alto line to a positive role in the proceedings, and his extempore fugues were apparently things of wonder, yet he did not seem to be able to translate this ingenuity into the printed form of his works for the organ, an instrument which is ideal for producing the clarity of texture required. The fugue of this work is an exception. All the parts, including the pedals, are given their full treatment, and Wesley successfully employs many of the contrapuntal devices available to him, to produce a movement that is a contrapuntist's delight.

Most of Wesley's organ works are available in modern editions, some of which present the works in a stylistic way; others, by voluminous fillings and other indiscretions, create a false impression of having been written for a large middle-aged instrument with heavy wind pressures. It must be said that Wesley's output for the instrument on which he was such a virtuoso is a disappointment, yet there are discernible influences in the early organ music of the English school which flourished at the turn of the century, especially in the works of such composers as Hubert Parry, Charles Stanford, Basil Harwood (1859–1949) and Edward Bairstow. These composers developed their organ music along different lines from the concert organists and composers such as Alfred Hollins (1864–1945), Henry Smart (1813–79) and others, who sought a secularising influence on organ composition, with all its platitudes and clichés. Wesley only strayed into this area with his early variations and to a lesser degree with his fashionable *Andantes*. In expressing some reservations about these organ works we must remember the limitations of the organs, coupled with the prevailing moods in cathedrals; these factors would have dampened the enthusiasm of a saint, and Wesley was less concerned with writing immortal music than creating a better situation for others to do so.

The Anglican Chant is a simple harmonised melody used for singing unmetrical texts, usually Psalms and Canticles. Although developed from the Gregorian Chant with its reciting note at the beginning of each line, it has a rather less flexible metre. The great vogue for writing chants, which is much more difficult than it might appear, reached its peak during the mid-nineteenth century. So many of them were badly written — poor tunes with maudlin harmonic support. On hearing a cathedral Evensong Dvorak is reputed to have enquired why the English are prepared to listen to such a bad tune sung so many times! Many will have shared his sentiments over the years. But few could cavil at S.S. Wesley's considerable contribution to the Anglican Chant. When he began his church career he would have found that normally the whole of the morning or evening Psalms would have been sung to the same chant, and that usually a single chant. The methods employed for changing notes were also varied, probably even chaotic. He protested vehemently and took practical steps to remedy the situation. These included writing a number of chants, the majority of them double, and, in his Psalter compiled for the Leeds Choir, he produced some of the earliest attempts at uniformity of movement by indicating where the words corresponded to the music. His chants are invariably interesting, the melodic line having a satisfying shape. A few were designed for congregational singing, but the majority were intended primarily for choir use, not least because of the wide range of melody employed. Even today Wesley's chants stand out for their exceptional quality, and there are many more available in the *European Psalmist* and the Leeds book of chants that are worthy of closer inspection. Dvorak would have held a different opinion if he had been listening to a Wesley chant.

Wesley was to invest English Hymnody with similar distinguished contributions. We have seen how he came to this new interest late in his career, practically all of his hymn tunes emanating from the Winchester and Gloucester periods. In view of the vast number of tunes that he wrote, it is surprising that only four have achieved universal success: *Aurelia* (The Church's one foundation), *Hereford* (O thou who camest from above), *Harewood* (Christ is our corner-stone) and *Alleluia* (Alleluia, sing to Jesus!), while others which are just as fine have lain in obscurity since their composition. In some ways it is a pity that *Aurelia* should be the most widely known of Wesley's hymn tunes for, by his own standards, it is rather ordinary, and is not entirely free of the less desirable excesses which beset the majority of hymn writers of that time. But it did bring his name before the church-going public as a composer who was able to bend his talents to their needs. Some of his tunes were written earlier, such as *Harewood* in 1839, but did not achieve particular celebrity for some time, almost certainly because they contained too many musical tricks to be understood, and were not too easy to sing. *Harewood* is a good example of this with its vital, leaping melody and the liberal use of longer notes, giving the tune great strength, but also an unfamiliar metre. It will probably come as a surprise to know that, in spite of its current popularity, *Hereford* was hardly known during Wesley's lifetime — or for many years afterwards. It is a miniature part song, for each of the lower parts, especially the tenor, are finely wrought to support this beautiful outpouring of melody. The lyricism and emotive expression are hard to find in any other hymn of the period. Another feature is that every line ends with a pure suspension, the 'feminine ending' which is a feature of all Wesley's work, but which here imparts a feeling of eighteenth century elegance. This is surely the most moving hymn tune that Wesley ever wrote.

The hymns detailed above give an indication of the three categories into which Wesley's hymns fall: the rather prosaic, functional efforts; the lyrical melodies, often in three measure and which are extensions of his shorter anthem style, and the more adventurous, even eccentric offerings. In almost all of his large output though there is rarely a hint of the corrupting influence of sentimentality, nor of triviality. Just occasionally his love for and knowledge of the German school shines through in his hymns: *Wigan, Bolton* and *Holsworthy* could so easily be mistaken for one of Wesley's tasteful harmonisations of a chorale melody by Schop or Schein. Through all his hymn tunes there is the mark of originality that places him apart from his contemporaries; above all he is not bound by their slavish adherence to regular patterns of harmonic sequences, especially at phrase ends. He is prepared to use a variety of cadences to suit his musical purposes, he is always ready to modulate to remoter keys, and to temper austerity in harmony with the subtler use of chromaticisms. In other words he was using the skills and techniques that he employed in his larger works to benefit the unlikely, restricted opportunities afforded by hymnody, and no one could dispute that he was successful. He deliberately set out to rival the efforts of his contemporaries, writing tunes to words that had already become wedded to someone else's forgettable endeavours. Wesley's tunes were never accepted as a viable alternative, and consequently such fine hymn tunes as *Orisons* or *Reliance*, both set to 'Abide with me', or *Kerry*, set to 'Sun of my soul' are unlikely to be heard. Another reason for the lack of use of his better hymn tunes is their association with words that were never in fashion. He thought deeply about the literary content of everything that he wrote, and hymns were no exception. He was generally not interested in the accepted hymnody of the church's seasons, choosing his words from a wide variety of general subjects. These unlikely subjects were to inspire him to write some of his finest tunes, sadly hardly ever heard. Many of these are in the minor keys, like *Leominster, Bath New* and *Dies Irae,* but the most regrettable loss to hymnody are the magnificent tunes like *Cornwall* and *Wrestling Jacob*, with their fine melodic line and inevitable leaning towards a minor key in the middle. Wesley's ability to create an uplifting point of climax in his tunes is a feature exemplified in all the above hymns, and is never more effective than in *Hereford*.

The *European Psalmist* is a fascinating book, and is well worth detailed study, for it tells us so much about Wesley's techniques as well as about his personality. His devotion to the German tradition is apparent throughout his selection. His dislike of the Gregorian traditions and the music of the early English School is just as evident by their almost total exclusion. His personal hatred of the hymns of Dykes and Monk and others is revealed by his inclusion of alternative original tunes or arrangements of just about every popular tune that was currently on offer by these gentlemen, even to the extent of arranging a tune by Spohr to cover 'Jesu, lover of my soul'. Many of these tunes and arrangements are good, but the odd one, like *Excelsior* for 'Onward, Christian soldiers', is too drab ever to be a possible alternative to the established tune by Sullivan. Another area of the book that is worth exploring is the skilful adaptations of melodies from anthems and other works. Such tunes as *Apostles* from Christopher Tye's 'O come, ye servants of the Lord' and *Penitence* from Richard Farrant's 'Lord, for thy tender mercies' sake' would make such a worthy, singable offering to our contemporary worship, in a way that so many of the pathetic 'modern' attempts at writing or adaptation palpably do not.

In some ways Wesley's adroit handling of hymn writing worked against him; too many were just too clever, containing more actual music than the average hymn singer could manage to absorb. He was especially adept at manipulating degrees of emotion through his tunes, but this was a subtle and cultured emotion that his contemporaries failed to understand as well as we do now. Not surprisingly many tunes are associated with his grandfather's words, although the Methodists were not too pleased with them, and they did not enjoy wide usage. Other tunes, including *Hereford*, have been matched with Charles Wesley's words at a later date, and it may well be that the composer would not himself have wanted them associated with the mood that they now have to convey through the arranged association. He himself thought carefully about the pairing of words and music in the tunes that he arranged from other sources, and some of these pairings are extremely successful. In the *European Psalmist* he brought to light a number of significant tunes that would really stand up well in our present-day hymnody, if only compilers and musicians would be more adventurous. Such a tune is *Eltham*, a remarkable little masterpiece from the eighteenth century. Used in one of the short reprints of the *Ancient and Modern*, it has long since been lost to sight, except that Parry used it for the second of his *Three Chorale-Fantasias* for organ, a work which has been described as "Parry's most perfect work for the instrument". Gerald Finzi (1901–56) continued interest in this work and the tune on which it is based by his exquisite orchestration of it for the Gloucester Festival of 1950.

In his lucid summing-up of S.S. Wesley's contribution to the English Hymn Tune from his book *The Musical Wesleys* (1968), Dr Routley writes:

> Some of his arrangements would strike an educated modern reader as hazardous, or even ham-fisted. Some of his original tunes are remarkably dull, and he shows little sense of how to rearrange for modern use any tune much older than *Eltham*. Some of his tunes are prickly and positively unpleasant. But where they are disagreeable to the ear, they represent that principle of dissent in him which made him sometimes an uncompanionable person, but none the less a brave and effective opponent of that supine conformity in which English church music was doing its best to suffocate itself.

This uneven quality of work to which Dr Routley refers can be traced through most of Wesley's works; even the great cantata anthems have at least one section that falls below the standard of the rest, and we have seen how often in his instrumental works he leads us on, only to disappoint. Yet he was always bold and courageous within the limitations of the Anglican church. He may not appear to be so advanced when compared with works being produced on the continent at that time, but he did develop his own inimitable style. He may have been influenced by Mendelssohn and Spohr, and gained inspiration from the works of Bach, but he was no plagiarist. He would have hoped that his music would have been considered English — a style that he personally forged to uphold and strengthen a great English heritage.

3.

His Writings

We have observed that the British religious scene was in some disarray, and that British music was in a depressing state of mediocrity. Cathedrals had largely avoided the problems of the former, but had readily accepted the condition of the latter. The insular nature of their existence had produced a moribund situation which extended far beyond the realms of music rendered at the statutory services. This indeed was the era of 'Barchester'. It was a disgraceful chapter in the history of our cathedrals and, although the musicians must share some responsibility, the clergy and those who supported them were most to blame. The overall authority for the life of the cathedral was vested in the Dean and his Chapter, who varied from three to six Canons; many of whom were rarely in attendance, and showed scant regard for the buildings or souls in their charge. Few had any musical inclinations, leave alone knowledge. Musicians were considered to be a necessary evil.

The cathedral organist and master of the choristers during the nineteenth century was frequently a local musician who 'did his best' under very trying circumstances; he was unlikely to be a person of any standing, certainly in the eyes of his employers, and he would more than likely have been despised by the social strata of those lay people who supported the status quo. Consultation with the clergy would not have existed; advice would not be sought, or given; encouragement would be rare indeed; reprimand would be a frequent occurrence. The cathedral organist would be near to the poverty line, endeavouring to survive by the endless round of mundane teaching, an activity hardly conducive to inspiring leadership from the organ loft. He would be isolated from his colleagues, who would themselves be 'ploughing their own furrow' within their own restricted environment. Cross-fertilisation of ideas would be non-existent, even in the unlikely event of there being any ideas to exchange. There were exceptions of course, but on the whole it was only in London that there were musical activities worthy of any attention, both in composition and performance.

The quality of life for the boy choristers under the direction of the organist was deplorable, and he was powerless to do much about it. Inevitably these appalling conditions would have an adverse effect on their singing, even if their master had the skills to train them, which could not be guaranteed in any event. His singing men would most likely be minor canons, clergymen who for the most part were not in the least musical, and were only too happy to evade their duties. One of the Church Commissioners of the time even assured members of the House of Lords that they "had no wish to tax the musical abilities of the minor canons"; this remark was followed by "laughter in the House". In places where lay clerks existed it would be extremely unusual to find even a minimum requirement, and more often there would not be enough singers to support all the parts. Their ability would also be open to question. Yet better singers would not be attracted to most cathedrals outside the London area, for the remuneration, in common with other church musicians, would have been abysmal. They could hardly be blamed for failing to turn up at choir rehearsals, and it was not uncommon for new music to be sung at sight during public worship, with disastrous results. There is also evidence to suggest that the music was often chosen while the service was in progress with the "indecency of boy choristers roving about with mess- ages". The chanting of the Psalms was shameful, the only discipline demanded being an approximate starting together at the beginning of the verse. Contemporary writers frequently referred to the irreverence of psalm singing in cathedrals, and in some places the words were so inaudible that it was doubted "whether they were uttered at all".

The general behaviour of choirs during worship was indes- cribable, as was their dress. Cassocks were not worn at that time, so the choir members appeared in any form of apparel, covered only by a surplice, which itself was usually torn and unwashed. Processions in and out of service were not normal, except on Festivals, the choir assembling casually and then distributing the music to be sung without any regard for those assembling for worship. By all accounts the spoken parts of the services were just as careless and inaudible, with the clergy showing as little regard for reverence as their musicians.

The boy choristers were generally boarded out with the master of the choristers or ecclesiastical dignitaries who lived in the environs of the cathedral. The provision of a home for the singers also carried the obligation of supervising their education and providing a decent upbringing, but this was rarely carried out. More often the boys were used for all manner of menial tasks about the house, dressed in tatters, neglected in matters of hygiene, and all-too-frequently treated with brutality. They were given little or no training in the duties for which they had been selected. The music was learnt by rote, and voice production was ignored; indeed, many boys continued to be members of the choir long after their voices had passed their usefulness. The exploitation and harsh treatment of children in mines and factories was well known and laws were eventually created to alleviate the problems, but people were prepared to disregard the unsavoury happenings in the idyllic settings of a cathedral close.

It is to be expected then that these unsatisfactory situations would produce poor standards, standards that were to deteriorate still more and be accepted by an ever-disinterested group of cathedral clergymen. The repertoire of the choirs became dire: works were repeated *ad nauseam*; the music sung and played was largely of a mundane nature, with little challenge or satisfaction being derived from performing it. In any event little money was available to buy new music or equip libraries with even the basic works. The organist often paid for music from his own meagre salary. It is on record that one cathedral organist said: "They [the Dean and Chapter] never spend a pound to purchase music; and if they did, the choir is in such a wretched state, we could not sing it".

From this distance of time it is perhaps difficult to imagine that things could be so bad and could be tolerated by people who were, after all, intelligent. But this serious state of affairs certainly existed and continued to do so for some time. There is even evidence to suggest that the apathy and downright antagonism by cathedral clergy towards their musicians existed into the present century, and some would even suggest that it is still not far below the surface. It probably has ever been so, for there is ample evidence of discontent from church musicians as early as the reign of Elizabeth I, and their fate during the Commonwealth period is well known. What is surprising, perhaps, is that the cathedral musicians were prepared to accept the situation with scarcely a murmur, until the arrival on the scene of Samuel Sebastian Wesley.

When Wesley chose a career in church music, rather than experiencing the brighter lights afforded by the London artistic scene, he must have been well aware of the problems that awaited him. If he had had any fears of a future in cathedral music, his work at Hereford and Exeter would have done little to reassure him. The distressing state of affairs would have been as bad at these two cathedrals as anywhere, and we have already referred to the plurality of the lay clerks at Hereford which caused him difficulties at the premiere of *Blessed be the God and Father*, and noted the excessive use of solo voices, rather than chorus work, in such anthems as *The Wilderness* — an indication, both of soloistic non-blending tendencies among cathedral singers of the time, and of insecurity of choral techniques. But at this stage in his career Wesley did not make any positive moves to express his disapproval of the organist's lot, except to absent himself with increasing frequency. This was the true 'opt out' of contemporary parlance. It was not until he was in the comparative security of Leeds Parish Church that he was prepared to exercise his literary skills on behalf of the subject that was so dear to his heart.

In his book *Cathedral Organists Past and Present* published less than twenty years after Wesley's death, John E. West (1863–1929) writes:

> Dr Wesley was a prominent advocate of reform in musical matters at our Cathedrals, and wrote and lectured with considerable insight and ability on the subject. But his efforts to obtain from the Cathedral authorities a larger amount of interest, and to place the musical service on a higher and more satisfactory footing, were only partly successful during his lifetime; and being a man of unusually sensitive temperament, it is more than probable that the many troubles and disappointments which he experienced in his Cathedral duties, helped in a great measure to shorten his days.
>
> There can be no doubt that these troubles largely accounted for the migratory character of his career as a Cathedral Organist.

It is a fact that at about the time of Wesley's move to Leeds some people were beginning to express disquiet at the poor state of cathedral music. As early as 1839 one John Peace published his *Apology for Cathedral Service,* in which he made many courageous statements on standards, as well as making some tactful suggestions for improvement. He also expressed concern that "men of another communion" (that is, Roman Catholics) were beginning to point the way towards more dignity in worship, which might result in prominent churchmen looking elsewhere for their spiritual satisfaction. Indeed, eight years earlier the magazine *Harmonicon* had expressed the following views:

> Who can doubt that the choral service of the Church of England would be one of the greatest feasts to be enjoyed on earth, if it were performed by educated musicians, with that unanimity which would result from their daily practising together? The Church of Rome owes much of her influence in this country to the wise attention which she pays to the performance of her music; it is grievous to see an unendowed sister surpassing us in a matter for which we are so magnificently provided.

Other distinguished churchmen such as Frederick Oakley and W. G. Ward also began to voice criticism, but the most pertinent comments were to come from the Irish priest, The Revd Dr John Jebb (1805–86), who undertook the vast survey of all the choral foundations in England and Ireland, publishing it with a flamboyant title so beloved by Victorians, of *The Choral Service of the United Church of England and Ireland, being an enquiry into the Liturgical System of the Cathedral and Collegiate Foundations of the Anglican Communion.*

Published in 1843 the book runs to seventy-nine chapters, in which the author examines in fine detail every aspect of his chosen thesis. Although criticism is not in any way restrained through the book, nor is Jebb afraid to name the offending cathedrals, his aims were to be positive and helpful. Cathedral administrations were left in no doubt that the responsibility lay firmly with them, and that they were not discharging their moral or legal obligations. Jebb was a personal friend of Walter Hook at Leeds and was invited to deliver three lectures in that city in 1841 on the same subject. These lectures were enthusiastically received, in no small way inspiring Hook to establish a 'cathedral-type' service at his Parish Church with the highest possible standards of attainment and dignity. As we have seen, S.S. Wesley figured in these plans. A year after Wesley had been in office at Leeds, Jebb published his *Three Lectures on the Cathedral Service of the United Church of England and Ireland*, a further indictment against the cathedral hierarchy. There can be little doubt that Wesley's own strong views would have been fired by Jebb's attack, although he would not necessarily have agreed with all the suggested solutions, and he probably felt that the time was right to follow up this lead with the first manifesto of his own campaign. The opportunity presented itself with the publication of his *Service in E major*, for which he was to write a rather fierce preface.

This first outburst was in some ways a miscalculation. The condensed nature of a preface did not give him sufficient room to justify his argument, so that the writing resembles a catalogue of carping comments. There is also a lack of continuity, suggesting that either he had not given the matter enough care, or he had not yet evolved a personal style of writing. In some ways it was a pity that he did not let the superb music that he had written speak for itself, for this was a most effective way of improving on the malpractices of his day. The *Service in E* is the end-product of his high aims; a practical step towards reform by a visionary who was himself setting a good example. The preface somewhat tarnished the image that the music could have created, but he was probably satisfied that he had made his point. He had 'nailed his flag to the mast'. The *Morning Post* branded him as "a Radical Reformer, a rater of the clergy, and particularly the dignitaries of the Church". Subsequent reprints of the Service wisely omitted the preface, but few were left in doubt that there would be more to come. They did not have long to wait. *A Few Words on Cathedral Music and the Musical System of the Church, with a Plan of Reform* appeared in 1849. This ample title covers a tract of seventy-eight pages, and although it is much more persuasive and carefully considered in its arguments than the preface, it still shows a certain immaturity in writing, not least in the length and number of footnotes. The book is well worth examining, for not only does it give a graphic description of cathedral music's ailments at that time, but it also provides an interesting insight into Wesley's own musical thoughts and preferences.

The first and greater portion of the book is devoted to a judgement on the poor state of cathedral music, the indifference of the clergy, and some suggestions for a "reformation" by the creation of professional standards. Wesley begins powerfully enough:

> A Bill relating to Church affairs will, it is said, shortly be brought under the consideration of Parliament, by which it is, among other things, proposed to reduce the Cathedral Choirs to the "least possible state of efficiency". Now, the Cathedral Choirs have long been in a state very far *below* one of the *least* "efficiency".
>
> It may appear too sweeping an assertion to declare that *no* Cathedral in this country possessed, at this day, a musical force competent to embody and give effect to the evident intentions of the church with regard to music; but such is the state of things, nevertheless.
>
> The impressions of either the occasional visitor or the regular attendant at Cathedrals, if analyzed, would afford nothing like well-defined criticism of the service, as a *musical* performance, which it really is; novelty in the one case, or the utter hopelessness of reform, or entire ignorance, in the other, serving either to palliate, or to exclude from all open complaint, that mass of inferiority and error which has long rendered our Church music a source of grief and shame to well disposed and well instructed persons.

He describes what the Cathedral Service is intended to be, stressing the need that there should be "competent performers, (or Ministers); secondly, the guidance of an able conductor, (or Precentor); and thirdly, that the musical compositions performed should be the emanations of genius, or of the highest order of talent. Such is the Church system". He points out that the demands of antiphonal singing require at least twelve men, with the addition of a few competent volunteer members. The singing minor canons receive his close attention, and he notes with alarm the ever-reducing number of singers in the cathedral choirs. "What", he writes, "can any one who visited the Opera Houses, the Theatres, Exeter Hall, or any well conducted musical performances, think of a chorus of *one* to a part? Ask the men working the mills of Yorkshire and Lancashire what they would think of it? And yet, this amount of chorus would be a vast *improvement* on the present state of things at Cathedrals; for there may be sometimes seen *one* man singing *chorus*!" Here follows the first of his many footnotes, an oft-told story of his visit to a service at Christ Church, Oxford.

> The writer remarked to the organist, Dr Marshall, "Why you have only one man in a surplice today, and him I can't hear". The reply was, "No, he is only a beginner". And this was in a University Town, where the first impression, as to the efficacy of Church Music, must be formed in the minds of young men preparing for holy orders, our future Deans of Cathedrals, to whom the character and fortunes of musicians become entrusted.

He then begins his attack on the clergy, who he describes as the "irresponsible directors of Cathedral music", and claims that any approach to them on the matter always produces the same result, "i.e. evasive politeness at first; then, abrupt rudeness; and ultimately, total neglect". In one of his most emotive footnotes he writes:

> Painful and dangerous is the position of a young musician who, after acquiring great knowledge of his art in the Metropolis, joins a country Cathedral. At first he can scarcely believe that the mass of error and inferiority in which he has to participate is habitual and irremediable. He thinks he will reform matters, gently, and without giving offence; but he soon discovers that it is his approbation and not his advice that is needed. The Choir is "the best in England", (such being the belief at most Cathedrals), and, if he give trouble in his attempts at improvement, he would be, by some Chapters, at once voted a person with whom they "cannot go on smoothly", and "a bore".
>
> The painter and the sculptor can choose their tools and the material on which they work, and great is the care they devote to the selection: but the musician of the Church has no power of this kind; nay more, he is compelled to work with tools which he knows to be inefficient and unworthy — incompetent singers and a wretched organ! He must learn to tolerate error, to sacrifice principle, and yet to indicate, by his outward demeanour, the most perfect satisfaction in his office, in which, if he fail, he will assuredly be worried and made miserable. If he resign his situation a hundred less scrupulous candidates soon appear, not one of whom feels it a shame to accept office on the terms, and his motives being either misunderstood, or misrepresented wilfully, or both, no practical good results from the step. His position, in fact, is that of a clergyman compelled by a dominant power to preach the principles of the Koran instead of the Bible.

This is obviously a description of his own experiences, and it would have made uneasy reading at the time. Neither would it be

98

encouraging reading for any young musician contemplating a career in the church, as Wesley expresses his fears that the superior attractions of the secular departments will attract men of genius and "careful education" away from the "Church School of Music . . . the highest of all schools".

There is then a quite lengthy discourse on the history of music in the English Church. This includes a brief historical note on the first English Prayer Books, together with the establishment of the Cathedral and Collegiate foundations. At this point some of the footnotes occupy more space on the page than the actual text, being mostly concerned with quotations from historical documents on cathedral music from specific choral foundations. Wesley eventually comes round to the view that church music was severely damaged by the Puritans, and appends two long quotations to support his assertions. He claims that the Church "has never recovered" from this period of its history, believing that Chapters still assiduously cling to the Puritan ideals. Here he again deplores the reduction of numbers in the choirs, stating that the downard path began at the time of the Reformation when "the Chapters had taken the Choir property into their hands". He points out that, in order to accommodate the much reduced choirs, composers have departed from the "true school of composition"; he expresses disgust that so many of the anthems and settings of canticles now being written for the church are not designed for choirs at all, but merely "exhibit particular singers". It should be remembered though that he was not disinclined to write soloistic anthems himself, vide *The Wilderness*. Wesley may have been inconsistent in this respect, but he most certainly did not sink to the depths of the glee-type church compositions, of which he was so critical. He suggested that this type of music was written more for the amusement of their author than out of deference for the Church, and opines that:

> Music like this has arisen partly from the decrease of Choirs, and partly from the Church having failed to acquire the services of eminent composers. The instances of a high species of composition being sung are very rare at any Cathedrals; while the performance of specimens which are contemptible is of daily occurrence at most of them.

He also expresses concern at the increasing influence of congregational participation, a result of "progressive" churchmanship. He claims that the mixture of "choral and parochial modes" is now commonplace, and is not consistent with a proper appreciation of the Choral Service:

> . . . and may not the propriety of making the congregation take prominent part in the ceremonial of religion be questionable, considering that it was not permitted for so many centuries in England, and that persons who take part in and perform a public ceremony, can never be so thoroughly imbued in spirit as those who preserve a silent attention? . . . it is surely one of the most beautiful attributes of Choral Service that the worshipper is not compelled at any time to utter anything to interrupt the prostration of mind which would ever attend a correct performance of that service in our beautiful Cathedrals.

In this historical section of his book Wesley makes a few inaccurate statements but, on the whole, his factual entries are sound and relevant to his argument, even if their effect is sometimes lessened by constant breaks in the flow in order to denounce yet another aspect of the clergy's incompetence or worrying theological trends. However, he does have the good grace to write that he doesn't really disparage the clerical office; he believes "a very large majority of the Clergy to be of the best of mankind". His argument, at least in this part of the book, is that "they have never recovered that just appreciation of the claims of Church Music, which they lost in the reign of Elizabeth".

Wesley considers that the strength of the 'Church School' lies in the fact of having "the best intellects of *many* centuries shut up in the religious and peaceful seclusion of Monastic Houses and *properly* given to its developement [sic]". He then goes on to question the quality of early British music compared with the "more distinguished masters" on the Continent. He makes disparaging comments on the works of Tallis, who he considers was unable to display the conception and breadth of such composers as Josquin des Prez or Ockeghem, although he does give him credit for writing some fine Responses! He does admit that Byrd, Gibbons and Weelkes, etc., are "worthy of study", but confesses that he had never seen an anthem by the latter. In his opinion though, Palestrina is in advance of all his contemporaries, and in

100

any event there are no grounds for believing that British music is anything other than inferior to its continental counterparts, especially the music of Italy, in spite of the boasts made in its favour.

> Whether the inferiority of England may result from the want of genius in our musicians, or the deficiency of encouragement from the powers that *were*, is a question. We see that, abroad, liberal inducements were extended to musicians, and the Art of Composition high prized. In England, Ecclesiastical Music, "No sooner born than blasted" . . .

He quotes from Martin Luther on the desirability of skills in music both for the schoolmaster and the ordinand, and then makes some random remarks on the "best specimens" of short anthems by John Farrant and Christopher Tye. Orlando Gibbons' madrigal *The silver swan* is accorded a special accolade, the writer regretting that it was not an anthem, for "it deserves a better fate than occasional performance by a Madrigal Society".

Although he shows some enthusiasm for the first Continental schools of church music composers, Wesley draws a line at anything earlier, especially the Gregorian tradition, which evoked from him the famous remarks I have already quoted. His venomous attack against the antiquarians ends with the remark: "This exalting the past upon the ruin of the present is unjustifiable". In a paragraph full of quotes from the Bible and Milton he rather unsuccessfully attempts to make his conclusions on this matter, but his arguments are inconsistent and, interesting as it is to have his views on music of an earlier age, this part of his treatise is little more than padding, and is largely the cause of a jaundiced view of Wesley by some musicians of a later, more 'enlightened' age.

In Wesley's plea for improved financial support for church music, as well as at a personal level, he recounts the case of the artist Landseer, who received a fee of a thousand guineas for a painting of a horse which, it is said, took him eight days to paint. He adds that

> were the musician who should produce a work of the highest merit in eight days, to ask, not a thousand guineas, but a thousand shillings, pence, farthings, the reply would be, invariable, "NO!" Let him study hard in his art, from the age of eight to thirty-five, sacrificing every interest to this one sole pursuit, let him offer his work as a present to *some* Cathedrals, and *they would not go to the expense of copying out the parts for the Choir!*

101

His experience at Exeter clearly still weighed heavily on him. Indeed, his disenchantment with his first two cathedral appointments is evident throughout, for he is very obviously speaking with a voice of experience. He resents the superior financial and musical status of the secular world of music, for he feels that church musicians are equal 'professors' in their own field — or should be. He cites the case of the support given to the Italian school of church composers, although he later contradicts it by saying that Palestrina died in poverty! But he is encouraged by the attempts being made to educate the population (he calls them the working class) in the rudiments of music:

> Knowledge of this kind, however, can work no good for the Church, unless its musical services become such as musically informed persons can respect. For otherwise: it may lead to very serious disturbances unless *results* be kept steadily in view.
>
> If the whole people be educated to appreciate fine composition and superior performance, as seems probable, and the Church, in her services, provides only what is revolting, must it not follow in due course that the people will seek some more correct and impressive performance of Divine worship themselves; and while their superiors are merely consulting, as they conceive, the *people's* tastes, and what is pleasing to *them*, the people, better informed, will take a nobler view of the matter and consider what is pleasing to GOD, and what it is their duty to bring before HIM.

Although he regrets that "public opinion, unfortunately, is rarely brought to bear on Cathedral music", he enthusiastically relates in detail the "remarkable exception" which had just occurred at Bristol. The Dean and Chapter there had elected to the office of Minor Canon a nobleman who could not sing and, as a result, the intoning of the service was abolished. This caused an outcry, and not only from the inhabitants of Bristol, for the event received full coverage even in such distinguished publications as the *Illustrated London News*. Eventually pressure was brought to bear on the Dean of Bristol to reverse his decision. How much of the pressure was concerned with upholding cathedral traditions rather than the British trait of supporting the 'underdog' — in this instance the genuine musical candidates for the post — is open to debate. Predictably Wesley enjoyed this particular battle and, after relating the affairs, he goes on to say:

The matter is here noticed in order to point to two facts of importance to the argument of these pages. One is the strong views exhibited by the Bristol public in favour of Cathedral service; the other, the most remarkable absence of all just appreciation of that service on the part of the Dean and certain members of the Chapter; one of whom avowed the very sentiments of the old Puritans who destroyed both Church and State, and murdered their Sovereign.

In the manner of a true reformer he loved a fight, but he was also at pains to point out that all these criticisms were made for the sole purpose of bringing an awareness of the threats to a national heritage, for which the church had a legal and moral responsibility. He is anxious to stress that his book does not advocate large or expensive rearrangements of the Church's affairs, nor does he attempt to discuss ceremonial.

All that is sought to be attained is a correct and decent performance of the Cathedral Services, as by law established; and to shew what are the very least means by which that object, at the present time, may be carried into effect. Music, assuredly, will ever form a leading feature in our public worship.

Towards the end of his indictment he questions why the church has not made a public appeal for help with its musical foundations, believing it to be distasteful for musicians to speak of money and religion in the same breath. His final plea before the setting out of his *Plan* is for the claims of music to be "as easily explained and understood as those of the comparatively simpler principles of architecture", which he believes the authorities were now recognising.

The solutions to the problems which he had outlined in length — *The Plan* — is quite brief, but the points are made strongly enough, and there are fewer breaks in continuity.

He begins by again highlighting the problems with lay clerks. He gives weight to his argument for at least twelve singers, with extras to meet absences. A two-tier system of payment should carry with it an obligation to attend rehearsals and be sufficient to encourage the lay clerk not to take on other employment. He advocates that in larger towns there could also be voluntary members of the choir. Leeds Parish Church was clearly his model for this statement, as his footnote reads:

> At Leeds, where the Choral Service is performed, and supported by voluntary contributions, several gentlemen attend on this footing, and with regularity and good effect.

He maintains that the lay clerks should be appointed by the cathedral organist, with the help of two other colleagues from the cathedrals near by. The quality of church musicians appointed as singers or organists would be much improved if a College could be established somewhere which would only be responsible for catering for the needs of church music. Wesley believes that this could be funded by those choral foundations who would benefit most from it.

He then turns his attention to the cathedral organist, who, he says, should in every instance be a "professor of the highest ability — a master in the most elevated departments of composition, and efficient in the conducting and superintendance of a Choral body". This latter statement was quite interesting, in view of his own known deficiencies in this department. He would hope that such a musician would have been trained at his proposed College, but this need not be the only criterion for appointment, the most important factor being to appoint men who are the "*bishops*" of their calling — "men consecrated by their genius, and set apart for duties which only the best talent of the kind can adequately fulfil". He again shows his regard for a collective appointments system, suggesting that the organist be selected by no less than seven of his colleagues. "In this, as in the case of the lay singers, there should be given to the Clergy a veto in respect to the moral and religious fitness of the candidate, and no more". He is very forthright about the salary associated with the appointment, pointing out that the "Cathedral Professor" should expect to be paid the equivalent of any *eminent* London musician, that is, in the range of £500–£800 per annum (perhaps even higher at St. Paul's Cathedral and Westminster Abbey).

His next subject is composition. He is anxious that the church should resume its sponsorship of the arts, in the manner of the continental church. He points out that the church musician has to depend on the vocal and instrumental materials provided for him by the clergy, whereas the sculptor or painter can acquire the quality of materials that he needs. Moreover, they and secular composers are more likely to be helped by the public, who tend to respond to a meritorious appeal. He gives Handel as an example of a composer who was able to write freely and successfully on account of the assured income provided by the state. He quotes in full Palestrina's pleading letter to Pope Marcellus, the point of the argument appearing to be the fact that at least he had someone to whom he could turn for help, and he did at least have a choir of sufficient skill to sing his music. This provides him with a further opportunity to enlarge upon the scandalous poverty of church musicians in Britain; he claims that they feel unwanted and lack any sort of security.

He then proceeds to other tools of their trade, recommending that the Cathedrals should have their own music copyist, and should give urgent attention to the organs; he speaks not only of their deplorable state of repair, but also of their correct siting for the best results of the choral service, drawing a plan to make his suggestions absolutely clear. As we have already noted, he was to write about this aspect of organ design and placing in much greater detail at a later date. He suggested that cathedrals should look at the possibility of installing a small organ for the accompaniment of the choir, with a large "noble" instrument somewhere else in the building, for instance, in the transept. This continental idea has never been accepted in this country, in spite of the obvious musical benefits afforded by it. All this, and the provision of printed music, should be administered by a specially elected "Musical Commission", which should also examine "the management of the Choir boys". This is the only reference that he makes to the children of cathedral choirs, yet he was painfully aware of the degradation of their status. Even though his Leeds arrangements for choristers were more civilised, if only for the fact that the boys lived at home, it would be surprising if he had forgotten the conditions at Hereford and Exeter. It would be equally surprising if he had felt no concern for the boys' welfare for, apart from his obvious devotion to his own children, there is nothing to suggest that he was anything other than considerate to the young people under his charge. They held him in awe, but were not afraid of him. Perhaps he felt that the cause being pursued with such vigour by Maria Hackett (the "Chorister's Friend") was sufficient, but the absence of comment in his book is puzzling nevertheless. He also makes the extraordinary statement that their [boys'] voices are a poor substitute for the vastly superior quality and power of those of women; but as the introduction of the latter is inadmissible, it is necessary to cultivate boys voices with due diligence.

In his gradual summing up he wishes

that the zeal, talent, order, and general good conduct of persons engaged in Theatres could be transferred to Cathedrals. In Theatres, talent is sure to be rewarded and error exposed, and punished by dismissal. The light of public opinion is, indeed, all-powerful.

He claims that

the country is not in such a state of destitution that Church worship cannot be adequately performed at our beautiful Cathedrals for want of funds . . . . From what has been here advanced it will be seen that but a very moderate increase of the present forces will, under proper musical authority, at least to ensure a daily performance, which shall both prove unexceptionable in itself, and cause the congregations of Cathedrals to delight in the services. So long as Choirs are maintained at their minimum state of efficiency, every objection on the score of unnecessary outlay must surely fall to the ground. Let it be borne in mind that a *minimum* state of real efficiency is all that is now being contended for.

Once place the music on a sound foundation, and, no doubt, assistance would flow in from many quarters, in aid of what would be found in the Cathedral towns one of the greatest public advantages.

Let us indulge a hope that the claims of this subject will find support, and that its merits will be better understood.

He ends with a final jibe at the clergy, who he suspects will view music "as a thing of secondary importance", but urges everyone to take the matter seriously, even to the extent of acquainting their members in Parliament of their concerns and wishes. His final words are:

The Choral Service, to be sure, has been shamefully neglected, and people who judge of it from what they have heard in Cathedrals, can form no high and adequate conception of the thing in its sublime reality, and must, therefore, feel a proportionably diminished interest in the object; still, better things are of no difficult attainment. The authorities, those who hold the scales, are not accused of anything worse than apathy, or want of taste: no settled atheism, which might lead them to reprobate Divine worship of every sort.

The book is dated Leeds, May 24th, 1849. But that is not the end. Wesley adds an appendix consisting of two motets by his father: an Antiphon *Tu es Sacerdos*, and a funeral anthem for men's voices *Omnia vanitas*. Wesley justifies the inclusion of these works by suggesting that they are "proof that talent in the highest order of Ecclesiastical Music can exist in modern times". He says that:

> if compositions for the church, like those of the late Samuel Wesley, are produced in this age, have we not ground for hope that, should the religious world arrive at a large and liberal appreciation of the subject, talent equally great, or greater, may be so far available, that each Cathedral may have its adequate share, and the compositions introduced into daily services become such as to warrant a national pride.

The style of writing throughout the treatise lacks fluency, a fact which Wesley acknowledges himself by craving indulgence from the reader in his preface; he admits that "his feeble and discursive *style* is not wholly unfelt by the writer himself"! His belligerent comments on the cathedral clergy are fascinating enough, even if rather repetitive, and certainly some of his arguments are expressed with persuasion and eloquence. Interesting as most of his comments are, they proved to have little effect during his time. It must be said that it was not a particularly influential document, although to us it presents some revealing historical facts and, above all, gives us a very good picture of the man himself.

Some of Wesley's suggestions were far-reaching and even prophetic, but he would have been realistic enough to accept the improbability of many changes being brought about during his working life. He would have rejoiced at the founding of the Royal School of Church Music, which in many ways reflects his ideas of a College for church musicians, especially as it was the brain-child — perhaps Wesley-influenced — of a cathedral organist, Sir Sydney Nicholson (1875–1947). Wesley would have been happy to observe the greater care afforded to cathedral organs, even if the siting would not always be to his liking; he would certainly have approved of the better status and ability of lay clerks, and we must assume that the strength of the chorister tradition, to say nothing of their education and welfare, would have given him enormous satisfaction. His hopes for the cathedral organist have not entirely been fulfilled. They are still required to undertake a vast amount of extramural work in order to make a satisfactory living; they are still not considered "professors" of their calling and, generally, funding of the musical foundation will not be anywhere near the sums that he suggested were necessary for their well-being. Wesley obviously looked with some suspicion and potential threat from the secular world of music, yet he could not have forseen that the high standards demanded by secular society would have had such a desirable influence on church music, particularly on the raising of standards of performance. Although much music has been written specifically for the church during this century, perhaps not all of the quality that Wesley would have hoped for, the church is still astonishingly reticent in commissioning suitable music — or, indeed, any other form of art. But the greatest joy of all for Samuel Sebastian would be the high esteem in which cathedral music, including his own, is now held by the public, both at home and abroad.

The *Few Words* was Wesley's major contribution to literature. He was again drawn into print in 1854 with his *Reply to the Inquiries of the Cathedral Commissioners*, but this pamphlet is more concise and says little that is new; indeed, it tends to follow the familiar pattern but with rather less conviction. This was to be his last document on cathedral music, although he did conduct occasional arguments on church and organ matters through the press. He was a fighter to the end, and was alone among his cathedral colleagues to have the courage, and the ability, to use his literary as well as his musical pen to bring to public attention the plight of their chosen profession. The great heritage of cathedral music is greatly in debt to him for that alone.

4.

His Times and Place in History

Samuel Sebastian Wesley is normally recognised as a typical product of the Victorian age. Yet he was born and spent his formative years at the time of the Regency, inheriting the characteristics of British artistic life, such as it was, from the Georgian period.

This was a period of exploration. Britain's mastery of the oceans had opened up new fields of trade as more and more areas were discovered and Anglicised. As communications became speedier, so speech became freer. Charles and John Wesley had proved that people were prepared to listen, that the spirit of adventure could be applied to matters of social concern. Religious bigotry was a force that had to be challenged. The new spirit of the age also embraced chemistry, science, physics and philosophy. It began to influence poetry and painting, as writers and artists began to question the traditional stylised forms and looked towards a more romantic naturalism. However, music had not made significant progress. The foreign dynasties on the British throne had brought their own brand of music and musicians, mostly centred on Italian opera, and the aristocracy were only too ready to support their monarch's whims, when they were not already engaged in pursuit of sporting activities. The national character was steadily being suppressed; the musical nation had lost its homogeneity; the public became more and more divided, with a huge mass of people relegated to insignificance and inferiority. However, restless spirits were abroad. They demanded freedom from formality, coupling this with a growing public awareness of indifference and exploitation. To the ruling classes this looked suspiciously like anarchy.

A few composers attempted to contribute to upper class entertainment by writing ballad operas based on folk music. They achieved a modicum of success, but their efforts were never likely to be a serious intrusion into the foreign dominance. A few others were still writing for the church, even though it was fast losing its credibility. These included two outstanding composers, William Boyce and Samuel Sebastian's own father, whose individual talents were great enough to overcome the general standard of mediocrity, although it took until comparatively recent times for us to fully realise it.

Wesley was born into a lifestyle which knew extremes of luxury and poverty, piety and propriety, lawlessness and dissipation. This was the era of club life, the popular music halls, new dances, balloon ascents, prize fighting, blood sports, and extravagances in most things, including the arts. Life was certainly not dull if you had money. It was a time of domestic pride in furnishing, decoration and house building or restoration; there was ardent support for the theatre, even if the actors were poor and the evangelicals had pronounced it as a decadent activity. Female culture was spreading, and there were rumblings of socialism. The divide between the ruling and working classes became even wider, touching every way of life, and inevitably having an adverse effect on cultural activities. The 'dark satanic mills' were real enough and necessary for national prosperity, or so the owners claimed. The real problem was that there were not enough mills to satisfy the people who wanted to work in them, thereby increasing hardships. The new England of William Blake's vision would be hard to build in the increasing climate of capitalism and industrialism. Although born into the Blake era, there was never any suggestion that Wesley was politically motivated, or ever felt moved to take up the cause of poorer members of the community, unless they were church musicians! Unlike most of his contemporary cathedral musicians he would most certainly have experienced the squalid life-style of the poor, as Leeds Parish Church at that time was surrounded by narrow, filthy, disease-ridden streets. He experienced a cholera epidemic at first hand.

The church, mostly in the persons of non-conformists, was questioning these conditions and the attitudes of the ruling groups, but the cathedrals continued in their own inimitable, cloistered way. The machinations and problems of the secular world were not for them. The clergy, usually products of Oxford and Cambridge, tended to be either scholars or antiquarians. They had become the social equals of the squire, and were anxious not to step out of line in political or community matters. One diarist of the time wrote that "English clergy are a learned, pious, moral and decent set of men, but not remarkable for professional activity". New prophets in their midst were soon condemned, for the "boat must not be rocked" in any way. So the agitators went their own way, with the result that new and exciting expressions of faith sprang up around the country. John and Charles Wesley had little choice but to take their ministry elsewhere. "The world is my parish", said John, as he travelled about a quarter of a million miles to preach over forty thousand sermons. The new movements had no heritage of music to draw upon, so they looked to a new folk-lore to aid their worship — hymn singing. This was a communal activity in which all could participate, and it cost nothing. Meanwhile the cathedrals plodded on, with ever-decreasing standards.

There would be no inspiration or directive from the government, nor from the monarch — and, anyway, he was insane. The Prince of Wales was appointed Regent a year after Wesley was born, acceding to the throne on the death of his father in 1820. In that period there was to be intense artistic activity in Britain, for these were the years of adventure and achievement. Walter Scott and Jane Austen were best-selling novelists with a new commanding style; Lord Byron and Percy Bysshe Shelley were poets seeking a new freedom of expression; David Garrick and Richard Sheridan held sway on the stage; Thomas Lawrence and Joseph Turner were at the peak of their considerable artistic powers, and John Constable was at last being accepted. But Prince George's real passion was for architecture, and much state money was lavished on grandiose schemes, usually prepared and carried out by his personal architect, John Nash. Most of these schemes were successful, and the end-products were to be a cultural asset to the nation. At the same time the Adam brothers began to instil new standards of building in London, giving a "sort of glory to the Regent's government which would be more felt by remote posterity than the victories of Trafalgar or Waterloo". The Regent also turned his attentions to his favourite watering-place, Brighton, inviting Nash to design the Pavilion and other buildings as a royal holiday retreat. We have already noted that Samuel Sebastian was

111

to experience courtly life in these new sumptuous buildings when still a boy chorister at the Chapel Royal.

None of this was likely to impress a country sinking deeper into the troughs of poverty and unemployment. The royal excesses were being questioned even in Parliament, where George III's sons were described by the Duke of Wellington as "the damned millstones around the neck of any Government that can be imagined". There began to be murmurings of discontent from the community at large: republicanism and radicalism were becoming commonplace topics of conversation. There was even an attempt upon the life of the Regent in 1817. Yet, on the whole, music was unaffected by these happenings, and certainly cathedral life was untouched by it.

At the time of Wesley's birth, the musical life of Europe was dominated by Vienna. As the adopted or actual home of the four great composers, Beethoven, Haydn, Mozart and Schubert, it could justifiably claim to be the capital of European music. Its influence would be slow to make much impression on British music, beyond the fact that one of its by-products, the Waltz, had taken a firm grip on the attentions of the pleasure-seeking groups. It was seen as yet another step into the morass of decadence. Even Byron was moved to write that "it [the waltz] wakes to wantonness the willing limbs". The waltz and kindred dance forms were to make their way into the popular theatre, and the young Wesley would certainly have come under their influence during his brief flirtation with the London stage. Whether or not he felt at home in the environment of this lighter music is hard to determine; nor is it clear why he decided finally to seek a career in church music, especially as he would have been well aware of its pitfalls. Perhaps he felt that his particular talents were restricted to this area of work; perhaps his family background had been an overpowering influence. Having made his decision he must have been determined to do all in his power to create a new and more promising musical world within the church by personal commitment and high standards of professonalism. His standards of commitment were to lapse all too frequently but his professional standing remained high to the end of his life. The brilliant standards displayed at the 1875 Worcester Festival when he was a dying man are ample testimony of that fact.

Wesley had moved in social circles enough to know that the upper and middle classes could afford to be patrons of the arts, if they were of such a mind. As the century progressed, poets, authors and artists could live by their works. The public enjoyed literature and paintings; they believed that the arts mattered. They felt the same about religion, but music as a handmaid to their religion did not grip their imagination and, as a result, their money stayed in their purses. Church music did not appear in their reasoning as a necessary form of patronage to appease their Maker.

The advancement of industry and the compilation of wealth from it was really their 'religion'. Britain boasted of being "the workshop of the world" when Victoria came to the throne in 1837. She had succeeded her father, William IV, (younger brother of George IV), who had reigned for seven years, during which time life had continued in the pattern enjoyed under the Georges. The monarchy was still unpopular, and even the young Queen's betrothal to Prince Albert of Saxe-Coburg-Gotha failed to arouse much excitement. Yet Prince Albert had much to offer. A man of many talents, he was to channel much energy into the arts and cultures of his adopted home. No mean musician himself, even if his attempts at composition would have been better left on the drawing board rather than in print, he did take an interest in the development of national music-making, in spite of the fact that this also took the form of encouraging too many foreign musicians to exercise their skills here, at the expense of indigenous talent. However, the Queen and her Consort were prepared to recognise home products, often lending their patronage to worthwhile musical undertakings. We will remember that these included the restoration of the Winchester cathedral organ under Wesley's guidance. The Great Exhibition had been the grand idea of the Prince Consort and resulted in some measure of appreciation by the public for his efforts, although the less-privileged were not to accrue many benefits from it. When Albert died in 1861, there was evidence of public regret, but he had never achieved the popularity that he probably deserved, and certainly for which his Queen had hoped.

In the meantime the German romantic movement had taken a grip on British music. The constant visits of composers and performers was having a devastating effect on musical growth, yet in other artistic ventures Britain was beginning to make an impression. The writings of Mrs Gaskell and Charles Dickens presented a courageous as well as distinguished approach, in an age when integrity was difficult, if not impossible, while the Brontës and others were making their powerful contributions to our literary heritage. Anthony Trollope, arguably the most able of all the Victorian novelists, was a man after Wesley's heart, although there is no evidence that they ever met, or that the composer had read the Barchester novels. But Wesley would have approved of Trollope's humorous and intriguing picture of life in the cathedral close; indeed, he could almost have written it himself!

There were also some notable paintings being produced, but an element emerged which considered that art here had become dangerously moribund. Forming themselves into a secret brotherhood, the Pre-Raphaelites claimed that the shallow and unrealistic artistic conventions currently favoured originated from the sixteenth century Italian master, Sanzio Raphael. They advocated a return to the medieval art form, with its taste for mysticism. Members of the group, never popular with the establishment, later turned their attention to church architecture, which they reckoned was suffering from a Germanising of Victorian England. The restored churches were being made neat and tidy, but lacked soul and atmosphere. Accusing fingers were pointed firmly in the direction of Gilbert Scott. This same Germanising was having an adverse effect on English music, so it is somewhat surprising that more musicians were not attracted to this movement. Sullivan was socially involved for a while, as were several performers, such as Joachim, but the absence of musicians from the Pre-Raphaelite movement was probably another indication of the poor opinion held by members of their sister art. Not that Wesley would have been specially interested as they were too devoted to medieval cultures. He had enough problems with the Tractarians for the same reason.

Exploration and empire building continued, as did the deepening division between rich and poor. In Wesley's lifetime internal disturbances included the Corn Laws, the Luddite and the Chartist revolts, the Cato Street conspiracy, the Peterloo massacre, and other lesser events, all of which confirmed that a new spirit of determination was springing up within the working classes against social injustice and exploitation. Elsewhere Karl Marx was propagating his new theories and the American Gold Rush was under way. War, if not in Britain itself, was an intermittent threat, with Waterloo, the Crimea and Bismarck's Germany marking the beginning, middle and end of Wesley's life. But the great achievement of the Victorians was the improvement of communications. Roads remained something of a problem, but the development of the steamboat, the building of canals, bridges and tunnels, and the invention of the iron road, all captured the imagination. Britain was particularly hit by a 'railway mania'.

And Wesley travelled quite extensively in Britain, mostly for the purpose of giving recitals. But it is something of a mystery that he made little effort to travel abroad. Musicians in the secular world relished their European connections, gaining enormous experience and a wider sphere of appreciation but, with their lesser talents, failed to bring anything new back to an expectant and improvingly perceptive audience. If Wesley had gained continental experience there can be little doubt that cathedral music would have derived great benefit from it. He might well have surprised the continentals too, by his own distinctive compositional techniques. As it is, his music is little known or appreciated in Europe.

Romantic influences in music were strong during Wesley's working life. There have always been romantic elements in music, but this was the time when self-expression and subjective emotion reached their most potent level. Composers were obsessed with painting pictures or telling stories through their music; there was a longing to be transported somewhere else, or to another age. This was the ideal climate for the development of music drama, and Verdi and Wagner were not slow to capitalise on it. It is extremely interesting to note that Wagner was beginning his opera-cycle, *The Ring*, in the same year that Wesley wrote his anthem, *Ascribe unto the Lord*.

The emotional language of the romantics was readily accepted into the music of the church, as it was into all aspects of ecclesiastical art and imagery. Used with discretion it was no bad thing, for the church was in desperate need of a new image to escape its dreariness. A change of emphasis in sensible hands could produce something of distinction for the benefit of the establishment. This Wesley most certainly did, but unfortunately so many of his contemporaries with inferior ability were only able to produce feeble works using less attractive elements of romantic language, thereby bringing church music into disrepute. Wesley's efforts were not exactly appreciated at the time, but for very different reasons.

Yet if Wesley had contemplated work experience on the continent he would probably have been just as disillusioned for, in spite of the great compositions emanating from all over Europe, the church on the whole was not a beneficiary of this inspiration. Traditional demands of the public liturgy and the romantic image were not really reconciled at this point in time. We need not concern ourselves with the vast corpus of music produced by the great composers of the nineteenth century under the general heading of church music, for the large scale Masses and Requiems are not part of the argument. But it is interesting to note what was being produced in Europe specifically for liturgical use. The Lutheran Church had virtually turned its back on the traditions established by J.S. Bach, even greater emphasis being placed on the spoken word so that the services resembled a 'chorale sandwich'. The Roman Church spent most of the century trying to reform its musical traditions, but without much success. Each country retained its own musical identity. Only the Germans came out of it with credit; but the French, led by the Belgian Cesar Franck and their own Camille Saint-Saens, were the most prolific. The Cecilian Movement was formed to forward the claims of the Palestrina school as the 'pure music' for the church, replacing the 'worldly' music for choir and instruments that had come into use during the previous century and now, in the hands of lesser beings, was creating an atmosphere that was seen to be bordering on vulgarity. Anton Bruckner and Franz Liszt were to produce some exquisite works in this recommended 'pure' style, making use of both Gregorian and modal features, but Mendelssohn was not similarly inhibited. He wrote several psalm settings in cantata-style, of which the famous 'Hear my prayer' is one (we might well wonder if Wesley knew of this), a number of motets, and even settings of the Anglican canticles. Most of the other established composers of the century wrote at least one piece of church music, except for Wagner, but these works would not have had wide circulation within the confines of the liturgy. A casual visitor to any place on the continent which had any sort of choral reputation would probably have been surprised and disappointed to find that the musical offering was little better than that found in Britain, with music composed by unknown occupants of the local organ loft. Our European counterparts advanced through their appreciation of the older masters. Conscious of the lack of creative spirit in their contemporary musicians they sensibly looked to the past. The Tractarians had similar ideas, but perhaps they looked back too far and, by doing so, failed to gain the interest of the musicians who could have helped their cause. Wesley's entrenched view on the earlier composers of the English tradition was ill-informed and damaging, and not really characteristic of someone who generally was well-read in musical matters and who would have had access to many of these masterpieces in libraries of the cathedrals in which he served. In any event, he was entitled to his own opinions. He was not the first composer to be critical of the Elizabethans, nor would he be the last, but he was misguided to be so outspoken on the subject when he was actually pleading for the cause of better musical standards in the cathedrals. It becomes obvious that, apart from a nod of approval towards the early Italian school, which he saw as being led by Giovanni Gabrieli, his musical appreciation really started with the music of J.S. Bach and continued through the music of his father.

His father's music was always a continual source of inspiration to Samuel Sebastian, and it cannot be denied that, even if most of it is written in an earlier style, it is very fine indeed. We cannot be certain how well Samuel taught his talented son, or what methods he used, but we must assume that the techniques of J.S. Bach would have been to the fore. Samuel's contrapuntal writing for voices is most felicitous; few would deny that his son inherited these skills, but he also progressed further, vesting his choral lines with a shape and emphasis to enhance the text in a way that had been rarely known before in English Church Music. This is one of his characteristics — a feature that makes his music instantly recognisable to a discerning listener. Another is his subtle use of chromatic harmony. It is easy to write that in this he was influenced by Spohr or Mendelssohn, but it would be kinder, and probably more correct, to say that he developed a particular language of his own, which was to influence other British composers later in the century. We never talk of Parry or Stanford being influenced by Spohr or Mendelssohn, although Brahms is often mentioned, yet when writing for the church the Wesley hallmarks can be detected, both in construction and in language. We know that Elgar was influenced by the methods and language of Wagner, among others, but we now only refer to his own distinguished and distinctive 'English voice'. Perhaps we should accord S.S. Wesley the same privilege and recognise his best offerings of church music as being a significant original voice in the 'wilderness' of nineteenth century English church music. Of course he had his faults — which composer has not? — and I have tried to acknowledge them, but the greatest regret that musical history must observe is that he failed to produce any instrumental music of any note. His father's brilliant example was not followed, nor does the devoted son make much mention of this aspect of the elder Wesley's skills. But it does cause one to speculate what might have happened if the younger Wesley had studied abroad, or been taken under the wing of one of the visiting composers. The talent was there, but for some reason the spark had never been fired. The same is true of writing a choral work on a larger canvas. How the Three Choirs would have loved a major work from him; we would probably still be performing it!

Wesley's music continues to promote controversy even among today's church musicians. It is possible to be completely captivated by his cultured and devotional style, with its emotional overtones; it is equally possible to find these same facets totally abhorrent. Other detractions are the claims that the writing draws too much from the common store of early Romantic slow-movement style, together with the protracted nature of so many works. His music may be loved or hated, but it cannot be ignored. I have experienced this so vividly during my own career, in which Wesley's music has of necessity and choice been ever-present. I have worked with an incumbent who went into a swift decline at the sight of a lengthy Wesley anthem on the music list, and a Dean who always contrived to have an out-of-town engagement when the composer's name appeared; yet both men, who were discerning musicians, requested *Thou wilt keep him* for their installations!

Throughout time demands have always been made that sacred art should have a recognisable ecclesiastical style. As we know, these demands have been met much less frequently than they have been voiced. We may sometimes be offended by the elaborate altar screen, or the extravagant decorations, or the over-colourful stained-glass, or the over-emotional portrayal of liturgy through words or music, but the generation that produced this style were offering to God the best of their art as they saw it at that time. Wesley was no exception, and no one can deny that his music was for the most part the best that he could possibly offer — and that it was much superior to anything else that was produced in the name of cathedral music over several decades of the nineteenth century. Perhaps he was not adventurous and tended to cling to an outmoded style with his cantata-like anthems, for certainly the verse anthem more or less died with him. It cannot be disputed that his best-loved anthems are those in a more concise form, while many fine hymn tunes and chants still await discovery. But behind all his music there is a power which could only have originated from someone who had devoted his life's work to the English Cathedral. In summing up Wesley's cathedral music in his centenary lecture of 1910, H.C. Colles wrote:

> It could not have been written by a man who was much concerned with the more strenuous aspects of artistic life. Whether they touch on the sorrows and aspirations of the human soul or the mysteries of faith, it is with a certain reticence which does not weaken their force, but rather strengthens it. They sum up Wesley's life-long convictions as to the function of Cathedral music. He saw in the cathedral service the means of contemplating in terms of art the deepest emotions and the highest aspirations of humanity. He found the existing organisation quite inadequate to its purpose, and he devoted his life to the realisation of his ideal.

These are profound words, but no less than Wesley deserved. He and his father were concerned for the future of church music in the nineteenth century in the way that their forbears had been concerned for the future of the church itself in the previous century. The family battled against philistinism in a way that had a lasting effect on the church and its music but, as we have seen, only Samuel Sebastian has ever fought as hard from within the ranks of cathedral musicians. He was revered by his colleagues, and his contemporaries referred to him as 'great'. He was undoubtedly a 'character' and there appeared to be some sides to his personality that were distinctly unattractive; but all good reformers are complex people, and he was no exception. For all the vigour that he displayed in his assault on the cathedral authorities, he probably died a disappointed man, for in all honesty he had witnessed little reform during his life. His efforts were to receive more attention and reward after his death. Cathedral music could have died in the nineteenth century. The fact that it survived was in no small way due to Wesley's courage and diligence.

In the year that Wesley died Alexander Bell invented the telephone, Colonel Custer fought his last battle, and Queen Victoria was created Empress of India. Wesley's achievements may well appear trivial by comparison, but in the history of British music he retains an outstanding and unique position. If the church had had more common sense to employ him correctly and to make better use of his gifts and wisdom he might well have enjoyed the reputation of some of the great musicians of Europe. Given those opportunities he might well have produced masterpieces in many musical forms. But his reputation must not rest on what might have been. He was indeed the last member of a notable family who made a tremendous mark upon English religious life. The maintenance and subsequent growth of Cathedral music to its present-day strength is in no small way a testimony to his perseverence, skill and perception. Samuel Sebastian Wesley was an extraordinary cathedral musician, and a genius.

Appendices

Appendix i

The Organist in Heaven

When Wesley died, the Angelic orders,
    To see him at the state,
Press'd so incontinent that the warders
    Forgot to shut the gate.
So I, that hitherto had follow'd
    As one with grief o'ercast,
Where for the doors a space was hollow'd,
    Crept in, and heard what pass'd.
And God said: — "Seeing thou hast given
    Thy life to my great sounds,
Choose thou through all the cirque of Heaven
    What most of bliss redounds".
Then Wesley said: — "I hear the thunder
    Low growling from Thy sea —
Grant me that I may bind it under
    The trampling of my feet".
And Wesley said: — "See, lightning quivers
    Upon the presence walls —
Lord, give me of it four great rivers,
    To be my manuals".
And then I saw the thunder chidden
    As slave to his desire;
And then I saw the space bestridden
    With four great bands of fire;
And stage by stage, stop stop subtending,
    Each lever strong and true,
One shape inextricable blending,
    The awful organ grew.
Then certain angels clad the Master
    In very marvellous wise,
Till clouds of rose and alabaster
    Conceal'd him from mine eyes.

And likest to a dove soft brooding,
   The innocent figure ran;
So breathed the breath of his preluding,
   And then the fugue began —
Began; but, to his office turning,
   The porter swung his key;
Wherefore, although my heart was yearning,
   I had to go; but he
Play'd on; and, as I downward clomb,
   I heard the mighty bars
Of thunder-gusts, that shook heaven's dome,.
   And moved the balanced stars.

A Tribute to the recently departed Samuel Sebastian Wesley by the Victorian poet, R. E. Brown (1830–97), who imagines his musical hero as organist in Heaven.

Appendix ii

The Organ at
Leeds Parish Church — 1842

Great Organ. 12 stops. Compass GG–F

1.	Front Open Diapason	8	
2.	Small Open Diapason	8	
3.	German Diapason	8	
4.	Stopt Diapason	8	
5.	Large Principal	4	
6.	Small Principal	4	
7.	Twelfth	$2\frac{2}{3}$	
8.	Fifteenth	2	
9.	Larigot	$1\frac{1}{3}$	
10.	Sesquialtera	3 rks	
11.	Trumpet	8	I. Swell to Great
12.	Clarion	4	II. Choir to Great

Swell Organ. 6 stops. Compass C–G

13.	Open Diapason	8
14.	Stopt Diapason	8
15.	Principal	4
16.	Hautboy	8
17.	Trumpet	8
18.	Cornet	9

Choir Organ. 8 stops. Compass GG–F

19.	Open Diapason	8	
20.	Stopt Diapason	8	
21.	Dulciana	8	
22.	Flute	8	
23.	Principal	4	
24.	Fifteenth	2	
25.	Mixture	4 rks	
26.	Bassoon	8	III. Swell to Choir

Pedal Organ. 1 stop. Compass CC–F

27.	Double Open Diapason	16	IV. Choir to Pedal
			V. Swell to Pedal
			VI. Great to Pedal

The Organ at Gloucester Cathedral — 1865

Great Organ. 11 stops.   Compass GC-F

1.	Open Diapason I	8	
2.	Open Diapason II	8	
3.	Stopped Diapason	8	
4.	Clarabella	8	
5.	Principal	4	
6.	Twelfth	2⅔	
7.	Fifteenth	2	
8.	Sesquialtera	4 rks	
9.	Mixture	2 rks	
10.	Trumpet	8	I. Swell to Great
11.	Clarion	4	II. Choir to Great

Swell Organ. 12 stops.   Compass C-F

12.	Open Diapason I	8
13.	Open Diapason II	8
14.	Stopped Diapason	8
15.	Dulciana	8
16.	Principal	4
17.	Flute	4
18.	Fifteenth	2
19.	Sesquialtera	3 rks
20.	Trumpet	8
21.	Hautboy	8
22.	Cremona	8
23.	Clarion	4

Choir Organ. 5 stops.   Compass G-F

24.	Dulciana	8	
25.	Stopped Diapason	8	
26.	Principal	4	
27.	Flute	4	
28.	Fifteenth	2	III. Swell to Choir

Pedal Organ. 1 stop.   Compass CC-E

29.	Pedal Pipes	16	IV. Choir to Pedal
			V. Great to Pedal
			VI. Great to Pedal

The two Great to Pedal may be a mistake with V referring to Swell to Pedal, or it may mean a coupling at 8ft and 16ft pitch.

Appendix iii

S.S. Wesley's
Principal Compositions

London Period

Orchestral:	Ballet Music	c.1825
	Overture in C	c.1827
Organ:	Variations on God save the King	1829
	Variations on an Air of Kozeluch	c.1830
Piano:	Waltz	1830
	The Witches' Rondo	c.1830
	Dance in D	c.1830
Sacred:	Gloria in E flat	c.1830
	Benedictus in A flat	c.1830
	O God, whose nature and property	c.1830
Song:	Young Bacchus in his lusty prime	c.1829
	You told me once	1830
	When we two parted	c.1831
Theatre:	The Dilosk Gatherer	c.1830

Hereford Period

Orchestral:	March in B flat	c.1833
	A Manuscript Overture	1834
Piano:	Three Pieces	1834
	Variations on an air of Bertini	c.1835
Sacred:	Sanctus in E	1834
	Blessed be the God and Father	1834
	The Wilderness	1832
Secular:	At that dread hour, (4 male voices)	1832
	I wish to tune my quiv'ring lyre (5 male voices)	1833
	Millions of spiritual creatures (Choir and orchestra)	1835

Song:	Blessed are the dead	c.1834
	By the rivers of Babylon	c.1834
	God moves in a mysterious way	1835
	I have been young	c.1832
	Oh, when do I wish for thee	1835
	Take thou thy son (Abraham's Offering)	
		1834
	The bruised seed	1834
	There breathes a living fragrance	1833
	The smiling Spring	c.1835
	Vital spark of heavenly flame	1835
	Wert thou, like me, in life's low vale	1832

Exeter Period

Organ:	Larghetto	c.1835
	Introduction and Fugue in C sharp	1836
	A selection of Psalm Tunes	1837
Sacred:	Blessed is the man that feareth	1840
	Hear thou in heaven	1840
	I will wash my hands in innocency	1840
	O Lords, thou art my God	1839
	To my request and earnest cry	1835
	Agnus Dei in E	c.1836
Secular:	When fierce conflicting passions (5 male voices)	
		1839
Song:	Did I possess the magic art	1836
	Orphan hours, the year is dead	c.1836
	There be none of beauty's daughters	1836

Leeds Period

Organ:	Two sets of Three Pieces for a Chamber Organ	
		1842/43
Piano:	March and Rondo	1843
	Jeux d'esprit, quadrilles a la Herz	c.1845
Sacred:	Morning and Evening Service in E	1845
	Cast me not away	1847

Winchester Period

Sacred:	Short Full Service in F	c.1865
	Chant Service in F	c.1849
	Deus Misereatur in F	1858
	All go unto one place	1861
	Ascribe unto the Lord	c.1852
	By the word of the Lord	1854

	Give the King thy judgments	1863
	I am thine, O save me	1857
	Man that is born of a woman	c.1849
	O Lord, my God	c.1850
	Praise the Lord, O my soul	1861
Secular:	Shall I tell you? (4 voices)	c.1851
	Ode to Labour (choir and orchestra)	1864
Song:	Almighty God, give us grace	c.1851
	For Charity's Sake	1860
	Most blessed Lord	c.1851
	O Lord Jesus Christ	c.1851

Gloucester Period

Organ:	Air with Variations: Holsworthy	
	Church Bells	1874
Sacred:	Chant Service in F	c.1868
	Chant Service in G	c.1870
	Deus misereatur in C	c.1868
	Gloria for 7 voices	1868/69
	Blessed be the Lord God of Israel	1868
	God be merciful unto us	1867
	I will arise	1869
	Let us now praise famous men	c.1873
	Lord of all power and might	1873
	O how amiable	1874
	The Lord is my shepherd	1875
	Wherewithal shall a young man	1875
Secular:	The Praise of Music	1872
	When the pale moon (4 voices)	1874
	Arising from the deep (5 voices)	1874

Date Unknown

Organ:	Fantasia: Andante Cantabile
	Andante in G
	Andante in E
	Voluntary
Piano:	Piece in C
Sacred:	Kyrie and Sanctus in F
	Kyrie in f sharp
	Sanctus in D
	Blessed is the man unto whom the Lord imputeth no sin
	Glory be to God on high
	Let us lift up our heart
	O give thanks unto the Lord

The face of the Lord
The Lord will give grace
Though round thy radiant throne
Thou wilt keep him in perfect peace
Wash me throughly
My soul hath waited long to see

Works by Wesley

Collections and Editions

Psalter with Chants	1843
Three Sacred Songs	1851
Twelve Anthems	1853
A Selection of Psalms and Hymns (Kemble)	1864
The European Psalmist	1872

Writings

Preface to the Service in E	1845
A Few Words on Cathedral Music	1849
Reply to the Inquiries of the Cathedral Commissioners relative to the Improvements in the Music of Divine Worship in Cathedrals	1854

Song

Silently, silently	c.1874
The Butterfly	c.1874

Bibliography

A. Herbert Brewer: *Memories of Choirs and Cloisters* (The Bodley Head), 1931.

H. C. Coles: *Essays and Lectures* (Oxford University Press), 1945.

E. H. Fellowes: *English Cathedral Music* (Methuen), 1941.

J. Jebb: *Three Lectures on the Cathedral Service* (Green, Leeds), 1845.

Kenneth R. Long: *The Music of the English Church* (Hodder & Stoughton), 1972.

J. Pearce: *Apology for Cathedral Service* (Bohn), 1839.

Kendrick Pyne: *English Church Music*, vol. 1, no. 5, 1935.

Bernard Rainbow: *The Choral Revival in the Anglican Church* (Barrie & Jenkins), 1970.

Eric Routley: *The Musical Wesleys* (Herbert Jenkins), 1968.

Percy Scholes: *A Mirror of Music* (Oxford University Press & Novello), 1947.

Watkins Shaw: *Three Choirs Festival* (Ebenezer Bayliss), 1954.

C. J. Stranks: *Dean Hook* (A. R. Mowbray), 1954.

J. Sprittles & W. Tweddle: *Leeds Parish Church* (British Publishing Council), 1960.

Donald Webster: *'Parish' Past and Present* (Leeds University), 1988.

J. E. West: *Cathedral Organists* (Novello), 1897.

The Annals of the Three Choirs (Chance & Bland), 1895.